THE CLASSROOM TEACHER'S GUIDE TO MAINSTREAMING

THE CLASSROOM TEACHER'S GUIDE TO MAINSTREAMING

By

ARLYN J. ROFFMAN, M.Ed., Ph.D.

Lesley College
Cambridge, Massachusetts

CHARLES C THOMAS • PUBLISHER
Springfield • Illinois • U.S.A.

Published and Distributed Throughout the World by
CHARLES C THOMAS • PUBLISHER
2600 South First Street
Springfield, Illinois, 62717, U.S.A.

This book is protected by copyright. No part of it may be reproduced in any manner without written permission from the publisher.

© *1983 by* CHARLES C THOMAS • PUBLISHER
ISBN 0-398-04786-3
Library of Congress Catalog Card Number: 82-19139

With THOMAS BOOKS *careful attention is given to all details of manufacturing and design. It is the Publisher's desire to present books that are satisfactory as to their physical qualities and artistic possibilities and appropriate for their particular use.* THOMAS BOOKS *will be true to those laws of quality that assure a good name and good will.*

Printed in the United States of America
CU-R-1

Library of Congress Cataloging in Publication Data
Roffman, Arlyn J.
  The classroom teacher's guide to mainstreaming.

  Bibliography: p.
  Includes index.
  1. Mainstreaming in education. 2. Handicapped children--Education. I. Title.
  LC4019.R63   1983   371.9'046   82-19139
  ISBN 0-398-04786-3

*Dedicated with warm appreciation
to my parents,
Bea and Larry Roffman*

**A flicker
of light
and the night
is gone
    thank you
    candle.***

------

*written by a student with special needs

Dear Classroom Teacher,

In recent years new special education laws have been enacted which have changed the scope of classroom education. Many state courts have ruled that every child has an equal right to quality education, regardless of his or her special needs, and the federal government has backed this concept with Public Law 94-142. Learning specialists are busily administering tests and making diagnoses; many offer prescriptions for the classroom teacher, but many do not.

This handbook has been devised for the classroom teacher who may not have extensive training in working with children with special needs. A number of learning problems have been defined, their manifestations described, and teaching strategies suggested. As special education is often longer on theory than on tangible suggestions for curriculum modification, I have tried to make the manual as practical as possible. You will find that most of the teaching strategies outlined can be easily incorporated into your present class format. Other strategies, however, may suggest significant changes in your style of presentation; changes that will perhaps be time-consuming at first, but which will ultimately make your teaching more efficient and more effective.

Attending to the individual strengths and weaknesses of your students will make a big difference in the learning environment that you create in your classroom. More individuals will succeed. I ask you to read the following pages thoroughly, plan any appropriate changes in your teaching style, and try once again with the students whom you have not been able to reach before. I feel certain you will see results.

Good luck!

Arlyn Roffman

INTRODUCTION

MAINSTREAMING: bringing the handicapped student out of the special, separate classroom into the mainstream of regular education to the maximum extent possible.
Mainstreaming is:
- providing each child with the most appropriate education in the least restrictive environment
- looking at the educational needs of special children rather than at their clinical or diagnostic labels
- seeking and creating alternatives to help general educators serve minimally handicapped children in the regular classroom
- uniting the skills of general and special education for the educational benefit of the children.

Council for Exceptional Children (1975)

A CONTROVERSIAL issue, mainstreaming has been the topic of hundreds of articles and texts since 1975, when the Education of All Handicapped Children Act (P.L. 94-142) mandated provision of the most appropriate education for all public school students in the least restrictive setting possible. Educators have been weighing the advantages and disadvantages of this mandate ever since, dissecting issues on both a theoretical and pragmatic level.

This manual leaves the arguments to others. It begins with an assumption that its readers are classroom teachers, who are open to integration of special needs students, but who are uncertain of their ability to adequately serve them. It aims to provide enough basic information to allow those same teachers to understand the individual needs of students and to try to meet them with confidence.

The following chapters focus primarily on the special needs of students with moderate learning disabilities, individuals who are likely to demonstrate several of the following

characteristics:
- significant discrepancy between the quality of oral and written work, with the former generally being considerably stronger.
- weaker ability answering essay questions than multiple-choice items on tests.
- considerable difficulty finishing assignments and tests within the standard time constraints.
- lack of consistency in the quality and legibility of handwriting.
- great difficulties in spelling.
  - spelling all words phonetically.
  - spelling words with reversals, such as *ded* for *bed*; and/or inversions, such as *was* for *saw*.
  - substituting similar-looking words for each other, such as *month* for *mouth*.
- weakness in oral reading.
  - reading totally by the phonetic approach.
  - reading with reversals and/or inversions.
  - substituting, omitting, or adding words while reading.
  - reading with a painfully slow pace and consequent lack of fluency.
- inability to deal with spatial relationships, such as those involved in charts, maps, jigsaw puzzles, or ring-toss games.
- inability to retain basic math facts; confusion with number sequences and/or abstractions.
- confusion with sequences, including the alphabet, months of the year, events in a story, directions to be followed.
- difficulties processing material that is presented orally.
- problems generalizing and integrating new information into the general bank of knowledge.
- weak response to skin stimulation (for example, difficulty identifying textures with eyes closed).

- inability to visually follow a moving object, such as a baseball or beam of light.
- poor body awareness and control, with difficulties using limbs and fingers appropriately in activities such as writing letters and numbers, playing an instrument, or catching a ball.

There are great numbers of students in classrooms throughout the country who display one or more of the weaknesses listed above. Some are learning disabled; others are not. Some manage to succeed despite their problems; others do not fare quite as well. *The Classroom Teacher's Guide to Mainstreaming* is designed to help teachers address the needs of any student who is faltering under the weight of his learning problems. The accent is on the *need*, not on the *label*.

In Section I the reader is introduced to those theoretical aspects of special education that are relevant to the stated purposes of this text. Chapter 1 presents the basic tenets of P.L. 94-142 and describes the full diagnostic-prescriptive process, from referral of a child for evaluation to implementation of the appropriate educational plan for that student.

Chapters 2 and 3 explain how students process information through their sensory modalities and how curriculum may be modified in order to fit the particular learning style of each individual in class.

Chapter 4 orients the teacher to the student's cumulative records. It suggests how to ferret useful information from the file and offers a brief introduction to several of the diagnostic tests that may have been administered to the child through the years.

In the fifth chapter the reader is encouraged to use informal diagnostic techniques to supplement the information offered in the cumulative records. Practical suggestions are offered to facilitate the use of informal assessment strategies within the classroom.

Finally, Section I closes with Chapter 6, which provides an

explanation and demonstration of how to use this handbook.

Several chapters follow in Section II. Each defines a specific learning problem, lists related observable behaviors, and offers suggestions for coping with that particular special need in the regular classroom.

The practical use of this manual is strongly linked to the use of the Observation Checksheet appearing on page xv. The reader is advised to photocopy this sheet and use it as a guide to the learning style of each classmember. This may be done by doing the following:

- listing the name of each student in the appropriate column;
- checkmarking problems that have been observed in class, as the chapters in Section II are read; and
- conferring with the Special Education teacher in school to confirm the diagnostic validity of these observations.

The completed checksheet will be a valuable resource to the classroom teacher, who, knowing that John Doe has a visual memory problem, can readily flip to page 82 in the handbook for a variety of appropriate teaching strategies.

Thus *The Classroom Teacher's Guide to Mainstreaming* offers practical support to classroom teachers. It strives to provide direct and personal assistance for planning the curriculum modifications needed to help special needs students thrive within the educational mainstream.

OBSERVATION CHECKSHEET

STUDENT'S NAME	distractability	impulsivity	hyperactivity	perseveration	weak automatization	inadequate auditory discrimination	weak auditory figure ground discrimination	auditory memory deficit	weak visual discrimination	weak visual figure ground discrimination	visual memory deficit	visual motor deficit	difficulties with visual-spatial relationships	conceptualization difficulties	difficulties understanding language	problems in expression	visual impairment	hearing loss

ACKNOWLEDGMENTS

MANY people have supported me as I have written the various drafts of this handbook.

Way back in 1974, when I was a resource room teacher struggling to orient my regular education colleagues to the complexities of new special education legislation, the Weston, Massachusetts Public Schools encouraged my preparation of the original manuscript. In the ensuing years the material was expanded in both quality and quantity as hundreds of teachers throughout the Northeast participated in my inservice training workshops and provided case examples and accounts of their own classroom experiences. I am particularly indebted to the many who so frankly expressed their frustrations and challenged me to brainstorm new approaches to mainstreaming.

I am grateful to Dr. Samuel Toto who acted as my mentor for many years and who helped with the writing of Chapter 1 on Public Law 94-142. I want to thank Janet Senzer for her critical eye as a reader of this final version. Thanks, too, to Mary Norberg for her endless patience as my typist.

I am particularly indebted to my friends and family for their support during the preparation of this final text. I would like to extend an especially warm note of gratitude to Pat Corey and Bill Greenberg for their loving encouragement all along the way.

CONTENTS

	Page
Dear Classroom Teacher	ix
Introduction	xi
Acknowledgments	xvii

Section I. Theoretical Aspects

Chapter		Page
1.	INTRODUCTION TO THE "EDUCATION FOR ALL HANDICAPPED CHILDREN ACT"	5
2.	LEARNING STYLES	9
3.	TASK ANALYSIS	17
4.	THE CUMULATIVE RECORDS	24
5.	INFORMAL ASSESSMENTS	44
6.	USING THIS HANDBOOK	49

Section II. Areas of Special Needs

Chapter		Page
7.	DISTRACTIBILITY	55
8.	IMPULSIVITY	58
9.	HYPERACTIVITY	60
10.	PERSEVERATION	63
11.	WEAK AUTOMATIZATION	65
12.	INADEQUATE AUDITORY DISCRIMINATION	68
13.	WEAK AUDITORY FIGURE-GROUND DISCRIMINATION	71
14.	AUDITORY MEMORY DEFICITS	73
15.	WEAK VISUAL DISCRIMINATION	76
16.	WEAK VISUAL FIGURE-GROUND DISCRIMINATION	79
17.	VISUAL MEMORY DEFICITS	82

		Page
Chapter 18.	VISUAL-MOTOR DEFICITS	86
19.	DIFFICULTIES WITH VISUAL-SPATIAL RELATIONSHIPS	88
20.	CONCEPTUALIZATION DIFFICULTIES	91
21.	DIFFICULTIES UNDERSTANDING LANGUAGE	94
22.	PROBLEMS IN EXPRESSION	96
23.	VISUAL IMPAIRMENTS	99
24.	HEARING LOSS	102
Appendix A.	A Final Note to Teachers	107
B.	Assessing Classroom Learning	108
Bibliography		113
Glossary		115
Index		119

THE CLASSROOM TEACHER'S GUIDE TO MAINSTREAMING

Section I
Theoretical Aspects

Chapter 1

INTRODUCTION TO THE "EDUCATION FOR ALL HANDICAPPED CHILDREN ACT"

SPECIAL education underwent a major revolution in the mid 1970s. Following Pennsylvania's lead in 1972, many states passed civil rights laws that promised quality education to all children, regardless of their education needs. Three years later, the federal government passed Public Law 94-142, "The Education for All Handicapped Children Act," reinforcing the concept that handicapped children should be educated with nonhandicapped youth to the maximum extent possible. Elaborate procedures developed to help school systems comply with these statutes are briefly described below.

Upon referral of a student by either family or school personnel, the child's past performance and present potential in learning environments is assessed. The evaluation process is unique for each student, individualized according to his or her presenting problems. Thus, specific assessment details for each referred student are carefully discussed and planned in a preevaluation conference attended by the Evaluation Team Chairperson, other requested professionals, the student's parents, and the child himself if he is at least fourteen years of age. The evaluation process must include a classroom assessment by the student's teacher and an educational history and current status assessment. Should the concerns of the parents and/or the Evaluation Team Chairperson suggest the possibility that the student may require a more restrictive program, further physical, psychological, and home environment assessments would be recommended. If appropriate, other specialists may evaluate the student as well. With written consent from the parents, data gathering commences.

The school nurse or social worker visits the home to obtain

crucial background information about the child's developmental history. Inquiries are made regarding prenatal development and birth; the timing of developmental milestones such as rolling over, walking, and talking; and the social and emotional adaptive behavior patterns of the child through the years. Parents are also asked to offer other potentially relevant data, such as history of early childhood illness or emotional trauma, or learning problems in other family members. In addition, parents may use this opportunity to discuss their own observations and concerns about their child. A written report of the home visit is submitted along with other reports when the team reconvenes to plan the appropriate course of action for the student being evaluated.

The classroom teacher describes the child's typical classroom performance, offering specific qualitative and quantitative data when possible. Classroom teachers are advised to log the behavior of students being evaluated, noting problems as they occur, e.g. briefly describing *when* and *how often* he speaks out of turn, and *what* he says. Patterns emerging from such an assessment often offer important diagnostic information, which frequently corroborates the findings of other team members. It is particularly important to note whether there is significant variation in the student's behavior between the home and school environments.

A physician examines the child for physical strengths and weaknesses and provides a written statement describing the nature of any constraints on the child's educational performance. Such constraints may range from obvious physical handicaps to subtle neurological damage.

The school psychologist/counselor, resource room teacher, generic specialist, speech/language therapist, vocational education teacher, and physical therapist perform formal and informal diagnostic procedures according to need. Reports from the above personnel generally include a description of available services and a recommendation of those that seem to be appropriate for the student being evaluated.

When the evaluation process has been completed, the evaluation team meets to review all assessments. Parents who question the findings of an assessment may request a second opinion by an assessor who has been approved by the school system at school expense, or by a specific assessor who is chosen by the parents at their own expense.

The information received during the evaluation is thus used to develop an Individual Educational Plan (IEP) for the student. The IEP includes a statement of the student's strengths and weaknesses and lists long-term goals in order of priority, breaking the latter into short-term attainable objectives. The IEP also lists specific educational services to be provided and the extent to which the child will be able to participate in the "least restrictive environment." Recommendations range from provision of the regular educational program with curriculum modification, to provision of a substantially separate program within the public school setting, to private school placement.

The student's Individual Education Plan (IEP) is discussed at a meeting attended by the IEP Team, which includes the parents. Following this meeting, a written copy of the IEP is sent to the parents for their approval. If the parents differ with the team's finding and the differences do not seem negotiable on an informal basis, the case may be sent to an impartial hearing officer for negotiation or, if all else fails, to civil court. If the parents are agreeable to the team's educational plan, however, they sign it and send it back to the school for prompt implementation.

The goal of the evaluation process outlined above is delivery of quality education to each student, regardless of the special needs that he or she might have. While special services are available in a supportive capacity in public schools, the major responsibility for implementation of Public Law 94-142 clearly falls on the classroom teacher.

The IEP generally offers a handful of suggestions to help instructors address particular learning problems uncovered in the course of the evaluation proceedings. Nonetheless, many teachers do not feel adequately prepared to provide appropriate instruction on a day-to-day basis for the student being evaluated. Therefore, it is the aim of this manual to ease the burdens of mainstreaming by acting as a further resource for individualized educational planning. The following chapters introduce some of the basic hows and whys of learning disabilities and offer specific strategies to facilitate the process of integration of special needs students into the regular classroom.

Chapter 2

LEARNING STYLES

EVERY learner has a personal style of approaching and mastering learning tasks. Some students acquire knowledge best through reading, while others absorb more from lectures. Some choose to study alone; others prefer to work in pairs or groups. Some mete out long-term assignments in daily increments, while others work best under pressure and wait until the deadline is at hand. Clearly there are differences in both the way students process perceptual information and in the way they personally approach learning tasks. It behooves the teacher to note these individual differences and to provide the accomodations necessary to allow maximum success for each student in class.

PERCEPTION

People learn by organizing and interpreting the raw data brought in through the senses. This process, called perception, is at the core of information acquisition. Each learner has his own individual perceptual profile, with visual and auditory strengths and weaknesses that often dictate how well he succeeds in learning situations. The visual learner, for example, may not function well in a lecture class; the auditory learner may not respond to lengthy reading assignments.

It should be noted that problems of perception are generally unrelated to problems of perceptual acuity. The child who has difficulty discriminating between the printed letters *b* and *d* may indeed have 20/20 vision. The student who cannot distinguish between the short sounds of *e* and *i* in the words *bid* and *bed* may well have perfect hearing.

No one is certain of the cause of perceptual disabilities, yet it is generally believed that 10 to 25 percent of all the students in our classrooms suffer from processing problems, or breakdown in modality functioning. Modalities are the channels through which people perceive and absorb new information. The channels are defined and explained below.

THE VISUAL MODALITY

The visual modality plays a significant role in school learning. Students are expected to read words and numbers, to discriminate between shapes, sizes, and colors; to copy notes from the blackboard. Within the broad scope of visual perception, there are several subskills:

Visual Discrimination

Visual discrimination refers to the ability to differentiate one object from another. Students are continually challenged to use their visual discrimination skills in classes. In science, for example, they must discriminate between a beaker and a graduated cylinder; in math, between the multiplication sign (×) and the addition sign (+); in English, as in all reading courses, between similar looking words, e.g. *mouth-month*, or letters, *b-d*; in French, between an accent grave (`) and an accent aigu (´).

Many students find it difficult to take note of the subtle differences between similar objects and fail to perceive the discrepancy between an *n* and an *m* in reading or between a half note and a quarter note in music. Such difficulties lead to decoding errors, to mistakes in writing, and to problems on assignments requiring the matching of identical or similar objects.

Although visual discrimination skills generally refine with maturity, problems do persist for many individuals. Students who struggle in this area may respond to visual perceptual exercises, such as discrimination drills or matching games.

In addition, most will benefit greatly from learning mnemonic tricks, e.g. regularly using the phrases "three bump m" and "two bump n" to remember how to form those letters in cursive writing, and other compensating techniques, e.g. reading a word twice, once with the confusing letter as a *b*, the other with the letter as a *d*, to see which works in the context of the sentence.

Visual Memory

Visual memory refers to the ability to store and retrieve that which is seen. The child who cannot remember what a word is supposed to look like may actually check his work again and again and never find a basic misspelling. He may forget how math examples are supposed to be lined up and miserably fail on a basic subtraction item. He is likely to have difficulty copying anything off the board and will often forget key items when asked to draw a person. People who forget faces, drivers who forget familiar routes, students who cannot play a decent game of Concentration, all suffer from visual memory problems.

Visual Figure-Ground Discrimination

Visual figure-ground discrimination refers to the ability to distinguish an object from its background. The student with a deficit in this area has trouble focussing on one particular item out of the thirty math examples on a page. He often cannot isolate and read a line of print, particularly if the sheet is in single-spaced type. He has a very hard time deciphering papers that have been mimeographed on both sides, has great difficulty finding someone in a crowd, and has trouble picking out Italy on a map of Europe. He is constantly distracted by irrelevant visual stimuli.

THE AUDITORY MODALITY

The auditory modality, too, is widely tapped in instructional settings. Students are expected to use auditory perception to recognize what they hear both in class and out.

A pure auditory experience eliminates all but information received through the ears. Listening to a lecture in class, to a recording of Winston Churchill's speeches, or to an announcement over the school's public address system are examples of tasks involving auditory stimulation. Without the benefit of lip movements to watch or outlines to read as visual reinforcement, the student must rely entirely on his auditory skills to receive the information. Because most people tend to be oriented less toward auditory than toward visual stimuli, tension typically mounts in the lecture class or language laboratory. The breakdown of auditory skills may come in any of the following areas:

Auditory Discrimination

Auditory discrimination refers to the ability to recognize the difference between sounds and to identify whether pairs of words like *pen-pin, watch-witch* are actually the same syllable twice or represent two different words. The name *Roffman* consistently coming across as *Rossman* on the telephone is typical of the type of mix-up occurring in auditory confusions. Somewhere in transmission, the frequency of the letter f is lost. Somehow, in transmission, the word *pet* actually does sound like *pit* to the person with difficulties in auditory discrimination. Students who have trouble differentiating between notes in music class; between similar-sounding words on spelling quizzes; and between rhyming and nonrhyming word pairs in poetry classes probably suffer from an auditory discrimination disorder.

Auditory Memory

The ability to store and recall what is heard is known as auditory memory. Students are commonly expected to remember the details covered in lecture classes, the definitions of orally explained vocabulary terms, and the wide range of oral directions delivered in school each day. Many tasks further require auditory sequencing, the ability to remember the order of orally presented material. The student with problems in this area will typically falter when given a sequence of oral directions. For example, when asked to open his math book, turn to page 20, and do item numbers 1-10, he may forget what is expected after the part about turning to page 20; or he may mix up the sequence, turning to page 10 and doing item numbers 1-20.

Auditory Figure-Ground Discrimination

Auditory figure-ground discrimination, another interesting subskill, is a term that refers to the ability to pick out necessary and relevant sounds from extraneous background noises. The child who cannot tune in to what the teacher is saying because he is distracted by the gym class next door, by the plane going overhead, or by the study group off in the corner is suffering from an auditory figure-ground weakness. Struggling, too, is the student who rarely understands films in French class because, seated next to the noisy projector, she tunes in to the hum of the machine rather than to the content of the movies. Such individuals are also likely to experience great difficulty concentrating when a teacher shouts an announcement over the din in the cafeteria at lunch; they simply cannot separate one voice from the background sounds of group chatter and clattering dishes.

MOTOR FUNCTIONING

A third modality is motor functioning. In addition to acquiring information through auditory and visual channels, individuals learn through the movement of body parts.

Fine Motor Coordination

Fine motor coordination refers to controlled manipulation of the fingers in activities such as handwriting, ball catching, and sewing. The child with fine motor problems is often unfairly teased by peers for his manual awkwardness and reprimanded by teachers for his persistently sloppy paperwork.

Gross Motor Coordination

Gross motor coordination requires controlled manipulation of the larger limbs in activities ranging from hopping and skipping to complex contact sports. The student who unintentionally bumps into desks in class; the one who consistently swings and misses when he is up at kickball; the one who trips over himself when he runs relays in gym is having gross motor problems. (Note: Fine and gross motor dysfunctions are not necessarily related. A child may be a fine skier, but be unable to tie a proper bow. Similarly, a child may be capable of beautiful handwriting yet not be able to execute a coordinated somersault.)

Tactile Stimulation

People also learn via tactile stimulation, feeling and discerning through touch. A child may grasp the concept of texture more easily by feeling the actual difference between sandpaper and cotton. Or he may finally understand the equivalence of 32° Fahrenheit and 0° Celsius when he feels water that has been measured at that temperature on both Celsius and Fahrenheit thermometers.

Movement or Kinesthetic Learning

Movement, or kinesthetic learning, is frequently interinvolved with the tactile modality. It allows a child to identify a letter traced on his back or to recognize an object placed in his hand even when blindfolded. Many children are taught the alphabet through kinesthetics, moving their hands over sandpaper letters, grasping their shape and motion through touch. Older students are encouraged to actually feel solid shapes in the study of geometry, or to manipulate models of molecules in the study of chemistry.

CROSS MODALITY

Most tasks involve more than one modality at a time. Students are expected to learn through various combinations of the visual, auditory, and motor channels. Two of the more common cross-modality combinations are discussed below.

Visual-Motor Tasks

Visual-motor tasks require coordination of the eyes and body. Jumping rope is an example of this, as is copying shapes off the blackboard. The child who struggles with copying may see the object correctly but be unable to transmit the visual message through the hand onto paper. He looks at the drawing, sees the image is not accurately transferred, yet does not know what to do to correct his error.

Auditory-Motor Tasks

Auditory-motor tasks require coordination of the ears and body. Clapping and dancing to the rhythm of music are auditory motor activities, as is taking dictation of nonsense syllables.

Summary

These then are the modalities. Just as each learner has his

own study style, he also has his own perceptual pattern and responds uniquely to modality input. It is up to teachers to recognize the differences among the individuals in their classes and to minimize failure by providing a balance of visual, auditory, and motor experiences in the day-to-day curriculum. This will allow each student to learn through his own unique pattern of strengths.

Chapter 3

TASK ANALYSIS

CLASSROOM teachers impose impossible demands when they expect success from all students on all tasks. As you have seen in the chapter on learning styles, one learner's strength is another's weakness. Thus, while three-fourths of the class may respond very well to one presentation format, the remaining quarter may falter and perhaps fail under the very same conditions. It is important that instructors look carefully at their teaching style and weigh the demands they make on their students. Is the balance weighted heavily toward auditory requirements in the standard lecture format? Are students required to learn from undiscussed assigned readings day after day? Is there a way to provide outlines and diagrams as visual backup in those lecture classes? And could class discussion supplement those assigned readings on a regular basis?

In order to meet the needs of those they instruct, teachers must be prepared to scrutinize their lesson plans and modify presentations and assignments according to varying capabilities. In the examples below, several assignments are examined with a necessarily critical eye:

Example 1

Ms. Smith announces to her seventh grade class, "We've discussed Lincoln's assassination for two days now. Tomorrow there'll be a quiz."

Ms. Smith is assuming strong auditory memory functioning among the classmembers. However, many students have difficulty following the pure auditory input of such a discussion, and they will fail the quiz. Ms. Smith could help these students remain focussed on the topic by introducing a variety of visual reinforcements such as pictures, flow charts, and basic outlines of the discussion.

Example 2

Mr. Jones asks his geometry students to copy several geometric shapes from the blackboard into their notebooks.

A number of students struggle with this task. The child with visual-motor problems miscopies the forms. While he may see each shape correctly, he is unable to transfer it with accuracy through his hand onto paper. The student with visual discrimination difficulties is unable to distinguish between an octagon and pentagon and he, too, miscopies the shape. The child with visual figure-ground problems struggles as well, due to his inability to focus on one shape at a time on a blackboard full of lines and angles.

Mr. Jones could alleviate the pressures on these students by planning for their individual needs. He could help the child with discrimination problems by providing plastic pieces in the shape of each geometric figure for him to manipulate and possibly trace. He could help the student with visual-motor difficulties by providing a mimeographed notebook sheet with the geometrics already drawn. For the child with figure-ground difficulties, he could isolate one figure at a time on the blackboard or mimeographed sheet.

Example 3

Ms. Corey surprises her class, "You've all read Chapter 4 on chemical reactions. We're having a pop quiz to see what you've gotten out of it." Ms. Corey falsely assumes that all of the students have been able to cope with the reading. Many, in fact, have been struggling with the very difficult vocabulary of chemistry and have had trouble understanding and remembering the facts. She could help them by discussing key terms prior to assignment of new readings and by reviewing key concepts in class discussions after all have individually read the material.

Example 4

Mr. Harvey tells his fifth grade class that they will be playing softball in gym this week and that he wants everyone to get up at bat at least once.

One child with visual problems has difficulty following the ball with his eye. He cannot connect the ball with the bat, and he becomes deeply embarrassed by his failures at catching out in the field. Another student, struggling with motor problems, also dreads the humiliation of this game. He has never managed to hit the ball before and has a history of consistently fumbling in the field. Mr. Harvey could help preserve the dignity of these students by requesting that they umpire or score for the team. Private remedial batting practice could be offered at another time.

Example 5

Mr. Greenberg invites his class to join him at their individual science tables, "I'm going to be at my table. I'll tell you what to do while I'm doing it. You follow, step by step."

Mr. Greenberg is offering a fine example of teaching through several modalities at once. Students with visual strengths may watch him as he performs the experiment, while those with auditory strengths may go on listening to the step-by-step description of the process. All are involved tactily as well. This is a triple-modality assignment and has a very high potential for success.

STRUCTURAL TASK ANALYSIS

Structural task analysis is a formal process through which teachers like those above may consider their instructional style, the ability of their students to respond as required, and the ways a task might be modified in order to address the vary-

ing strengths of individuals in class. Noted in the process are such factors as the following:
 (1) task instructions — whether instructions are delivered orally or in print; whether they are clear or vague; whether they are given in simple units or in a complex series of steps.
 (2) input/presentation mode — whether the information is presented through visual, auditory, or kinesthetic channels or through any combination of these modalities.
 (3) output/response mode — whether the student is expected to provide a verbal or motor response or a combination of both.
 (4) level of difficulty — where the task falls on the continuum of learning tasks.
 (5) criterion — the level of acceptable performance, e.g. 80 percent correct in a period of one-half hour.

McLoughlin and Lewis (1981, p. 182) offer an excellent example of formal structural analysis in Figure 1.

A SAMPLE OF FORMAL STRUCTURAL ANALYSIS

Task: Given a list of 10 spelling words read orally by the teacher, the student will write the correct spelling for at least 8 of the 10 words.

Instruction: A series of verbal directions from the teacher: "Get out a sheet of paper and number from 1 to 10 along the left-hand side. I'm going to read your spelling words to you, and I want you to write them on the paper."

Presentation Mode: The student must listen to verbal input (oral language).

Response Mode: The student must recall a series of letters in correct order and write the series correctly.

Criterion: The student must correctly spell at least 8 of the 10 words.

Ways to Modify the Task:
 1. Reduce the number of words that must be spelled.

2. Reduce the criterion for acceptable performance.
3. Modify the instructions so that fewer directions are given at one time.
4. Modify the input mode from verbal to visual. For example, the student could view two different words, one spelled correctly and one incorrectly, and attempt to choose the word that is correctly spelled.
5. Add visual input to the verbal input. For example, the student could listen to the word while viewing two spellings of the word, then attempt to choose the word that is correctly spelled.
6. Modify the output mode from motor to verbal. For example, the student could spell the words orally.
7. Modify the output mode from writing to pointing. For example, if the student is shown several possible spellings of the words, the response could be to point to the correct version.

Figure 1. A Sample of Formal Structural Analysis. From McLoughlin, James A. and Rena B. Lewis: *Assessing Special Students: Strategies and Procedures*, Indianapolis, Bobbs-Merrill, 1981

A teacher may use this form of task analysis to examine and modify lessons of every sort. While the process may seem time-consuming at first, with practice it will flow more readily and may easily become part of a teacher's instructional planning activities.

FUNCTIONAL TASK ANALYSIS

There is a second format through which instruction may be evaluated. Functional task analysis considers the sequence of subgoals involved in the assignment of any one task. By identifying the numerous smaller demands that a task may make on a student, the teacher is helped to prepare the learner to meet each greater goal, step by step.

Ideally in a learning situation, the student begins with all the skills and concepts needed to proceed through the series of steps leading to achievement of the instructional objective. Unfortunately, students are often quite poorly equipped to meet the demands of an assignment and literally get lost in the mire of the undifferentiated subtasks involved.

By breaking down a larger objective into clearly differentiated, achievable subtasks, the teacher creates an assignment that offers greater opportunities for success in learning. The student proceeds through one step at a time, meeting success at each level, until the final goal is achieved quite naturally. For example, for Tony to learn how to write his name in manuscript, he must master the following sequence:

1. recognizing his name in print
2. conceptualizing the movements necessary to write his name
3. copying his name with free movements, with a model
4. writing his name with free movements, without a model
5. writing his name from memory, with the restrictions of a #2 pencil

His teacher, aware of the sequence of subtasks involved in teaching a child how to write his name, asks Tommy to do the following:

1. Look at a clay model of the name "Tommy"
2. Trace the model with his fingers
3. Looking at the model and his paper, trace over his name written in solid lines, using a thick marker
4. Trace over his name written in dotted lines, using marker
5. Print it himself with a marker, with a printed model of the name available before him
6. Print it himself with a marker, from memory
7. Print it from memory with a pencil.

By the time he arrives at the point of independently printing his name in pencil, Tommy is able to approach the task with confidence. He carries all the cumulative good feelings of his interim successes as he proudly prints his name. His teacher has allowed him to take the sequential route, and this is just what Tommy has needed to succeed in this task.

Thus, task analysis is an extremely important part of individualized teaching. Through the use of this technique, an instructor may look critically at each assignment in class, analyzing the full sequence of subtasks involved and identifying which modalities have been tapped. With this information and an understanding of learning styles, the teacher may confidently modify his curriculum and thereby begin to truly meet the individualized needs of those students in his class.

Chapter 4

THE CUMULATIVE RECORDS

THERE are times when a teacher, wanting information about a student, finds no specialist available for quick consultation and turns to the cumulative records for educational data and history. Unfortunately, most schools never weed out the second grade handwriting sample or the inconsequential note that Billy's parents once wrote to the counselor when Billy was ten years old. The teacher is faced with a thick folder, not knowing where to start reading or which data to trust.

It is, of course, impossible to write a comprehensive chapter on reading cumulative records, as each school system uses a unique method of record keeping and its own battery of tests. Yet it *is* possible to offer some general suggestions and an overview of some of the more commonly used diagnostic measures.

Suggestions:

(1) Look carefully at the family data generally appearing on the front cover of the folder. Often it is of vital importance to realize that this is one of nine children, that the father was recently deceased, or that the parents have each remarried after divorcing from one another three years ago. Note the student's grades over the years, checking his performance record against the date of any family trauma. Note whether he slipped academically after the death or divorce in his history and whether he ever regained lost ground.

(2) Try to establish a sense of the reasons for the onset of the student's problems by looking for patterns in the academic grades he has received since entry into the classroom at age five. For example, problems that sur-

face and continue from grade one may be developmental in origin, whereas patterns of difficulties that emerge in junior high school may be related to the biological and social changes of puberty.

(3) Cross-check grade patterns with the student's attendance records over the years. Note numbers of absences, the time of year when they occurred, and the grades that followed each period of extended absence.

Winter absences suggest chronic upper respiratory infections and, possibly, a subsequent hearing loss.

A history of extended absences in the early years suggests that the student may have missed considerable instruction in the basics and perhaps has never managed to catch up with his grademates.

Chronic absence over several years suggests school phobia, major health problems, or lack of parental support for regular school attendance.

(4) Check the number of schools the student has attended. A history of numerous transfers suggests a lack of continuity of instruction and exposure to a confusing mixture of teaching techniques. Both impede academic success.

(5) Examine the medical history that also appears on the front of the folder.

Note whether the student should be expected to wear prescriptioned eyeglasses. Many young people refuse to wear them and subsequently suffer an inability to succeed at boardwork.

Check, too, for childhood diseases that may have affected the student's hearing or sight. Note that an Rx history of Ritalin® or Dexedrine® suggests a diagnosis of hyperactivity has been made in his past. Note whether the student is on Dilantin® or phenobarbitol for seizure control. While chemical interventions such as these are often extremely helpful to the child, occasionally side effects and/or an outdated prescription will account for behavior or learning problems that arise in school.

(6) Skim through teacher and guidance reports from the student's early years. Note that the reading disabled eighth grader who had trouble learning the letters in first grade has had eight years of frustration with the written word. The same is true with numbers and math. If the teacher is able to empathize with this frustration, he will be in a better position to recharge the student's motivation for yet another year of remedial activities.

(7) Note the date of any IQ score included in the folder. A fourteen-year-old whose last intelligence evaluation was completed in second grade deserves a retesting before any further judgement is made of his abilities.

Of the many IQ tests used in schools today, the individually administered seem to be the most valid. The *Wechsler Intelligence Scale for Children — Revised (WISC-R)* is perhaps the most commonly utilized of these individual measures. Administered and interpreted by trained professionals, the *WISC-R* assesses intellectual functioning by sampling performance on several different types of tasks including verbal comprehension, arithmetic reasoning, and visual-motor tasks. The examiner scores and interprets the test results, generally reporting his findings in writing and inserting them into the student's folder. Such reports are usually straightforward, describing the student's Verbal (V) and Performance (P) strengths and weaknesses and providing important information to back up the simple number that comprises the Full Scale (FS) IQ score. The categorizations in Figure 2 are suggested by the *WISC-R* designers for interpretation of this Full Scale intelligence quotient.

It is important that teachers realize that while these numbers provide a useful guideline for classification of

WISC—R INTELLIGENCE CLASSIFICATIONS

IQ	CLASSIFICATION
130 and above	Very Superior
120-129	Superior
110-119	High Average (Bright)
90-109	Average
80-89	Low Average (Dull)
70-79	Borderline
69 and below	Mentally Deficient

Figure 2. WISC-R Intelligence Classifications. Reproduced by permission from the Wechsler Intelligence Scale for Children — Revised Manual. Copyright ©1974 by The Psychological Corporation. All right reserved.

learning potential, they represent only a portion of the information yielded by *WISC-R* testing. It is generally wise to read the examiner's narrative accounts of the testing sessions. These describe the student's anxiety level and testing style and suggest reasons for possible variations among subtest scores.

Formal Reports of Evaluation Procedures

Many cumulative folders contain diagnostic tests that have been administered by specialists but that have not been fully interpreted on paper. The tester may have verbally transmitted the information to the appropriate fifth grade teachers, who may even have managed to alert the sixth grade teachers as the child moved on. Nonetheless, all too often, by the time the record has arrived at the junior high school, the bare test protocol is all that remains of the evaluation. Generally, this is of little use to the classroom teacher who is unfamiliar with formal diagnostics.

Formal reports of evaluation procedures are an extremely important component of the student's record. They provide invaluable information regarding the individual's behavior during testing sessions. A good report describes the student's response style: What was the period of hesitancy between the time when he was asked a question and when he responded to it? How much did he respond? How did he answer questions when he did not know the answer? When he did know the answer, did he respond by speaking or by using gestures? How well did he attend to the tasks? Did he need continual reassurance as he went along? Were there apparent problems with visual or hearing acuity? Was he hyperactive . . . or lethargic?

Such observations provide highly practical informal assessment information which may actually be of greater assistance to the teacher in instructional planning than some of the "harder" data from standardized tests. Teachers are, therefore, encouraged to read these reports with considerable care when they are available.

Standardized Tests

Unfortunately, detailed write-ups are less commonly found in student folders than they should be. More often, the classroom teacher will find an array of standardized test results which describe the student's abilities in the form of grade levels, age levels, percentiles, or stanines. These norm-referenced standardized tests, while limited in diagnostic scope, do provide useful information. They sample student behavior under standardized conditions, allowing comparison of one student's test performance to the performance of a normal group of age or grade peers.

The remainder of this chapter is devoted to orienting the classroom teacher to several of the diagnostic instruments more commonly used in assessment batteries, and often appearing in cumulative records.

Detroit Tests of Learning Aptitude

The *Detroit Tests of Learning Aptitude* (Baker & Leland, Bobbs Merrill Co., 1959) are used to determine the learning style of students aged three through adulthood. Although the complete set of nineteen sections is never given to any one student, the specialist is able to learn a great deal by choosing a selection of subtests which fit the needs of the particular student being evaluated. Figure 3, from the authors of the *Detroit* manual, offers a task analysis of each subtest in the *Detroit*.

Test	Reasoning and Comprehension	Practical Judgment	Verbal Ability	Time and Space Relationships	Number Ability	Auditory Attentive Ability	Visual Attentive Ability	Motor Ability
1. Pictorial Absurdities	x						x	
2. Verbal Absurdities	x		x					
3. Pictorial Opposites							x	
4. Verbal Opposites			x					
5. Motor Speed and Precision		x						x
6. Auditory Attention Span for Unrelated Words						x		
7. Oral Commissions		x			x	x		x
8. Social Adjustment A	x							
9. Visual Attention Span for Objects							x	
10. Orientation	x	x		x				
11. Free Association			x					
12. Memory for Designs				x			x	x
13. Auditory Attention Span for Related Syllables						x		
14. Number Ability					x			
15. Social Adjustment B	x							
16. Visual Attention Span for Letters							x	
17. Disarranged Pictures	x			x			x	
18. Oral Directions		x				x	x	x
19. Likenesses and Differences			x					

Figure 3. Detroit Tests of Learning Aptitude: The Tests and Specific Mental Faculties. From the *Detroit Tests of Learning Aptitude,* by Harry J. Baker and Bernice Leland, Indianapolis, Bobbs-Merrill, 1967. Copyright© by Harry J. Baker and Bernice Leland.

DETROIT TESTS OF
LEARNING APTITUDE
For all ages from three
years through adult ages

Detroit Tests of Learning Aptitude
(Individual)

PUPIL'S RECORD BOOKLET

Copyright 1935 by Harry J. Baker and Bernice Leland
Revised 1959
The right to modify or print this work for use in the
Detroit Public Schools has been assigned to the
Board of Education, City of Detroit.

Name.. Sex............ Case No............
Date............................ School................................ Grade 7
Birthdate.................... C.A. 12-4 Med. M.A. 10-2 I.Q. 91
Time Started................ Finished.................. Examiner...............

No.	Test	Score	Age	Rank	Interpretation
1.	Pictorial Absurdities				
2.	Verbal Absurdities				
3.	Pictorial Opposites				
4.	Verbal Opposites				
5.	Motor Speed 2' 3' 4'		9-9	6	Very weak motor ability and/or judgement
6.	Auditory Attention Span for Unrelated Words Simple Score / Weighted Score		8-6	8	Very weak auditory attention
7.	Oral Commissions				
8.	Social Adjustment A				
9.	Visual Attention Span for Objects Simple Score / Weighted Score		13-2	1	Strong visual attention and memory for objects
10.	Orientation				
11.	Free Association 1' 2' 3' 4' 5'				
12.	Designs		11-0	4	Possible weaknesses – visual memory, motor, time-space orientation
13.	Auditory Attention Span for Related Syllables		11-4	2	weak auditory attention
14.	Number Ability				
15.	Social Adjustment B				
16.	Visual Attention Span for Letters		10-1	5	weak visual attention and memory for letters
17.	Disarranged Pictures				
18.	Oral Directions		9-8	7	Possible weaknesses – auditory memory, motor, judgement
19.	Likenesses and Differences		11-3	3	weak verbal ability

Summary of Impressions...............................

Figure 4. Detroit Tests of Learning Aptitude: Sample Protocol. From the *Detroit Tests of Learning Aptitude*, by Harry J. Baker and Bernice Leland, Indianapolis, Bobbs-Merrill, 1967. Copyright© 1935 by Harry J. Baker and Bernice Leland.

A typical middle school *Detroit* protocol is offered in Figure 4. The student's chronological age (C.A.) is 12-4, or twelve years, four months. The test scorings indicate that his median mental age (Med. M.A.), the age at which he is functioning, is 10-2 years. His computed IQ is 91.

The Age and Rank columns next to the subtest listings are considered by the test authors to be of great importance. They suggest that the digits under Age represent the actual mental age level at which the student functioned on that particular subtest. Thus, on test #5, for example, this student demonstrated the practical judgement and motor ability of a child nine years, nine months old. However, it is the opinion of this author that the Age scores should be treated more as *indicators of tendencies* in learning than as precise measures of age level functioning.

The Rank column offers a quick reference to the student's strengths and weaknesses. His strongest score ranks #1, with the subsequent ranking of all administered subtests. According to the results of this test, for example, this student is strongest in visual attention and memory for objects and weakest in general auditory attention. Therefore, his teachers would be wise to present visual reinforcement in chart, diagram, or demonstration form for any oral presentations made to this student.

Wepman Auditory Discrimination Test

While most appropriate for use with children five to eight years old, the *Wepman Auditory Discrimination Test* is sometimes implemented to diagnose gross discrimination problems in older students as well. Designed to determine ability to recognize differences among sounds in English speech, the *Wepman* requires students to listen to forty pairs of words and to indicate whether the examiner is pronouncing two different words or the same word twice, e.g. *tub-tug*. A score of four or more errors by a middle school student indicates that auditory discrimination may be a problem and suggests that further testing is desirable.

Note: Results of the *Wepman* must be interpreted with caution, since there is little information offered about its standardization sample. Therefore, this test is typically used as a screening rather than as a hard and fast diagnostic device.

The Peabody Individual Achievement Test (PIAT)

The *Peabody Individual Achievement Test* (Dunn and Markwardt, 1970) assesses several areas of academic achievement: math, reading, spelling, and general information. On each subtest students are shown a test plate with four possible responses for each item. No writing is required on this test, and reading is only required on subtests assessing spelling and reading achievement.

AGE DATA

Date of testing ___ (year) ___ (month) ___ (day)
Date of birth ___ (year) ___ (month) ___ (day)
Age at testing 9 (years) 0 (months)

TEST SCORES   Grade 3.5

NORMS RECORDED (Check one) .... ☐ Age ☒ Grade

SUBTESTS	Raw Scores	Equivalents	Percentile Ranks	Standard Scores
Mathematics	34	3.3	42	97
Reading Recognition	19	1.3	1	65
Reading Comprehension	21	2.1	9	80
Spelling	17	1.2	2	69
General Information	29	3.9	6.0	104
Total Test	120	2.3	19	87

Figure 5. PIAT: Sample Protocol. From the *Peabody Individual Achievement Test,* by Lloyd M. Dunn and Frederick C. Markwardt, Circle Pines, Minnesota, American Guidance Service, 1970.

Two sets of norms are available to the examiner, making it possible to compare the student's performance against his peers' by either age or grade. The *PIAT* is appropriate for individuals in grades K-12, from 5.3 to 18.3 years of age.

In Figure 5 the third grader tested is well below grade level in Reading Recognition, Reading Comprehension, and Spelling. His total test score is, therefore, quite low, despite Mathematics and General Information scores of approximately normal grade level.

The *PIAT* is one of the achievement tests most frequently used in assessing strengths and weaknesses in school learning.

The Key Math Test

The *Key Math Diagnostic Arithmetic Test* (Connelly, Nachtman, and Pritchett, 1971) is an individually administered test designed to provide an assessment of skill in mathematics. Yielding a grade equivalent score based on total performance on fourteen subtests, it identifies patterns of weakness in the areas of content, operations, and applications. *Content* includes basic math knowledge and concepts; *Operations* is the term applied to basic computation skills; and *Applications* refers to the ability to use both content and operational skills. The test also describes skill objectives for each item sampled.

This diagnostic instrument is used primarily in grades K-9, but there is no upper limit for individual remedial use.

The Wide Range Achievement Test (WRAT)

The *Wide Range Achievement Test* (Jastak, Bijou & Jastak, 1978) is a three-part test divided into two levels. Level I is designed for use with children 5 years, 3 months (written 5.3) to eleven years, eleven months (11.11) old. Level II is for those aged 12.0 to adulthood. Each level includes three subtests:

34 The Classroom Teacher's Guide to Mainstreaming

Figure 6. WRAT: Sample Spelling Protocol. From the *Wide Range Achievement Test* by Joseph Jastak, Sidney W. Bijou, and Sarah Jastak, Wilmington, Delaware, Jastak Associates, 1978.

Spelling, Arithmetic, and Reading.

Figure 6 provides a sample *WRAT* spelling test. Although the student is very nearly twelve years old, he has been dictated the list from Level I in order to provide him with a more successful testing experience. He has scored 43 points, giving him a grade rating of 5.3 (3rd month of 5th grade). While this formal score clearly indicates that the student is considerably below grade level in spelling, the list itself offers further informal information on the child's strengths. His adequate copying of the line forms and his neat reversal-free writing suggest adequate visual-motor functioning. His consistently phonetic spelling indicates strong auditory discrimination, while flagging a possible visual memory deficit.

The math subtest of the *WRAT* yields a grade level score but offers little definitive diagnostic information on the student's math-related strengths and weaknesses.

WIDE RANGE ACHIEVEMENT TEST — JASTAK

Page 4
Reading, Level I — A R Z H I Q S E B O 10
Two letters in name (2) — A B O S E R T H P I U Z Q 25

cat see red to big work book eat was him how 36

then open letter jar deep even spell awake block size 46

weather should lip finger tray felt stalk cliff lame struck 56

approve plot huge quality sour (soun) **imply** (implay) **humidity** (hŭmidy) **urge** 64

bulk exhaust abuse (abust) **collapse glutton clarify** 70

recession (rēcision) **threshold horizon** (her'ĭ zan) **residence** (DK)=(don't know) **participate quarantine** 76

luxurious rescinded (rē sin ded) **emphasis** (em phī'sis) / **aeronautic** (arnic) **intrigue** (in' trigee) **repugnant** (rēnant) 82

putative (poot) **endeavor** (DK) **heresy** (DK) **discretionary** (DK) **persevere anomaly** 88

rudimentary miscreant usurp novice audacious mitosis 94

seismograph spurious idiosyncrasy itinerary pseudonym aborigines 100

Level I.
Raw Scores (RS)
and Grade Ratings (GR)

SEE MANUAL FOR NORMS

RS	GR	RS	GR	RS	GR	RS	GR	RS	GR	RS	GR	RS	GR	RS	GR	RS	GR	RS	GR	RS	GR
0	N.7	9	P.6	18	K.6	27	1.5	36	2.3	45	2.8	54	3.8	63	5.1	72	6.6	81	7.6	91	8.8
1	N.8	10	P.7	19	K.7	28	1.6	37	2.4	46	2.8	55	3.9	64	5.3	73	6.7	82	7.7	92	9.0
2	N.9	11	P.8	20	K.8	29	1.7	38	2.4	47	2.9	56	4.0	65	5.5	74	6.9	83	7.9	93	9.2
3	P.0	12	P.9	21	K.9	30	1.8	39	2.5	48	3.0	57	4.1	66	5.7	75	7.0	84	8.0	94	9.3
4	P.1	13	K.0	22	1.0	31	1.9	40	2.5	49	3.1	58	4.2	67	5.9	76	7.1	85	8.1	95	9.4
5	P.2	14	K.1	23	1.1	32	2.0	41	2.6	50	3.2	59	4.4	68	6.0	77	7.2	86	8.3	96	9.5
6	P.3	15	K.2	24	1.2	33	2.1	42	2.6	51	3.3	60	4.5	69	6.2	78	7.3	87	8.4	97	9.6
7	P.4	16	K.4	25	1.3	34	2.2	43	2.7	52	3.4	61	4.7	[illegible]	[illegible]	79	7.4	88	8.5	98	9.7
8	P.5	17	K.5	26	1.4	35	2.2	44	2.7	53	3.6	62	4.9	[illegible]	6.5	80	7.5	89	8.6	99	9.8
																		90	8.7	100	9.9

Figure 7. WRAT: Sample Reading Protocol. From the *Wide Range Achievement Test* by Joseph Jastak, Sidney W. Bijou, and Sarah Jastak, Wilmington, Delaware, Jastak Associates, 1978.

The reading section, requiring the student to decode as many words as he can, yields a fair assessment of the student's word attack skills. Examination of the test booklet itself (Figure 7) indicates that this boy's word attack skills are very weak indeed, that he tends not to use the phonetic approach when reading, and that he becomes quickly frustrated when faced with polysyllabic words. No information at all is yielded regarding the boy's ability to comprehend what he reads.

The Gilmore and Gray Oral Reading Tests

Both the *Gray Oral* and the *Gilmore* Tests assess oral reading skills by asking the student to read aloud as quickly and accurately as possible several selections of graduated difficulty and length. The examinee is marked off for omitting or adding words, for substituting one word for another, or for repeating words or phrases as he reads.

Therefore, valuable diagnostic information regarding reading rate, accuracy, and comprehension is available through use of either *The Gilmore Oral Reading Test* (Gilmore & Gilmore, 1968) or *The Gray Oral Reading Test* (Gray, 1963).

Figure 8 indicates that Jimmy Selleck is a strong, fast reader. His decoding accuracy and his comprehension of content paragraphs are both above average.

The Woodcock Reading Mastery Tests

The *Woodcock Reading Mastery Tests* (Woodcock, 1973), a set of five subtests designed for use in grades 1-12, measure several reading skills. The subtests, which may be administered individually, in combinations, or as a full set, are briefly described below:

LETTER IDENTIFICATION TEST. The student is shown rows of individual letters and must say the name of each. Letters are uppercase and lowercase, manuscript and cursive, and dif-

The Cumulative Records

NAME _Jimmy Selleck_

TEST SUMMARY   Form C

PARA-GRAPH	ACCURACY ERRORS	ACCURACY 10 MINUS NO. ERRORS	COMPREHENSION NO. RIGHT (OR CREDITED)	RATE WORDS IN ¶	RATE TIME IN SEC.
1		10	5	24	
2		10	5	45	
3		10	4	50	
4	1	9	3	73	23
5	3	7	4	103	41
6	6	4	3	117	47
7	9	1	2	127	52
8	12	0	2	161	
9			1	181	
10				253	
	ACC. SCORE (TOT. "10 MINUS NO. ERRORS" COLUMN)	51	COMP. SCORE (TOT. NO. RIGHT OR CREDITED) 29	(1) NO. WORDS READ° 420 (2) TIME IN SEC.° 163	
STANINE		8	7	(1) ÷ (2) 2.6 × 60	
GRADE EQUIV.		7.8	6.7	RATE SCORE (WPM) 156	
RATING		Above Ave	Above Ave	fast	

→

Figure 8. Gilmore: Sample Protocol. From the *Gilmore Oral Reading Test* by John V. Gilmore and E.C. Gilmore, N.Y., Harcourt Brace Jovanovich, 1968

ferent type styles.

WORD IDENTIFICATION TEST. The student is shown rows of isolated words and must name each. There are no time limits.

WORD ATTACK TEST. The student is shown rows of nonsense syllables and words and must name each. There are no time limits.

WORD COMPREHENSION TEST. The student is shown a row containing three words, representing an incomplete analogy (such as "mother — big:baby — "). The student must read the three words silently and say a word that correctly completes the analogy.

PASSAGE COMPREHENSION TEST. The student is shown a line drawing and a sentence describing the drawing. One of the words in the sentence is missing. The student must read the sentence silently and say a word that would correctly complete the sentence. More difficult items present a sentence without a drawing.

In each subtest the student looks at each item in an easel-style standing test notebook and orally responds.

The *Woodcock* yields several subtest and total test scores that can be quite confusing to interpret. It is recommended that classroom teachers focus on just three of the many possible types of scores:

(1) the Reading Grade Scores indicate the student's instructional level.
(2) Percentile Ranks allow comparison of the student's performance with that of grade peers.
(3) Relative Mastery of Grade Placement estimates the student's reading performance in relation to the demands of the grade in which he or she is enrolled. This score yields valuable information for decision-making regarding mainstreaming of handicapped students.

McLoughlin and Lewis (1981) note the importance of

analyzing not only individual subtest scores but also subtest scores relative to one another. For example, they suggest that it is useful to compare the results of the Word Identification and Word Attack subtests in order to contrast sight vocabulary and phonics skills. They further note that the Word Comprehension and Passage Comprehension subtests are interesting to compare, particularly as they do not measure traditional reading skills. The Word Comprehension Test, presenting incomplete analogies, tests reasoning as well as vocabulary. The Passage Comprehension Test, requiring the student to complete sentences, focuses on context clues rather than on the more traditional skills of drawing conclusions or general comprehension.

The *Woodcock* is one of the reading achievement tests most frequently used in the assessment of special needs students. Results from this test add a wide range of valuable information in diagnostic evaluations of a child's reading skills.

The Gates-MacGinitie Reading Test

The *Gates-MacGinitie Reading Test*, 2nd edition (MacGinitie, 1978), is a two-part test measuring the student's vocabulary and comprehension. Several forms are available for use at the various grade levels, K-12. Norms are provided for three testing times during the year: October, February and May.

The vocabulary subtest assesses the student's reading vocabulary and is more a test of word knowledge than of decoding skills. Items consist of test words characteristic of those likely to be read by students in the grade range covered by the test. These are followed by five words or phrases; the closest in meaning to the test word is chosen by the student.

The comprehension section measures the student's ability to read complete prose passages with understanding. Items represent a range of content from published sources. Questions graduate in difficulty from basic recognition to inferential thinking.

Figure 9 presents a case sample of a sixth grader who is below average in vocabulary and comprehension. His raw score of 26 on the vocabulary subtest falls in the fourth stanine and earns a percentile rank (PR) of 35. This means that his raw score is higher than 35 percent of the students at the same grade level and, in turn, is lower than 65 percent of his grade mates. His grade equivalent (GE), or grade level, in vocabulary is 5.3. His reading comprehension is at the 32nd percentile rank, at a grade level of 4.7.

Scores	Raw Score	Stanine	NCE	PR	GE	ESS
Vocabulary	26	4		35	5.3	
Comprehension	22	4		32	4.7	
Total	48	4		33	5.1	

Student _____ (Last name, First name)
Grade 6 Date October Form D-1
Teacher _____
School _____
NCEs and percentile ranks based on norms for
October X February ☐ or May ☐ of grade 6

Figure 9. Gates-MacGinitie Reading Test: Sample Protocol. From the *Gates-MacGinitie Reading Test,* 2nd edition, by Walter H. MacGinitie, N.Y., Teachers College Press, 1978.

Readers interested in the use of the NCE (Normal Curve Equivalent) Scores and/or the ESS (Extended Scale Scores) are referred to the test manual.

The Illinois Test of Psycholinguistic Abilities (ITPA)

The *Illinois Test of Psycholinguistic Abilities* (Kirk, McCarthy, and Kirk, 1968) is often used with children 2.4 to 10.3 years of age to assess communication difficulties in three cognitive areas:

(1) channels of communication (both input and output)
(2) psycholinguistic processes (reception, association and

expression)

(3) levels of organization (representational and automatic)

Scores yielded by the *ITPA* provide an age equivalent called the Psycholinguistic Age (PLA) and Scaled Scores. Total test scores include the Composite Psycholinguistic Age and a Median Scaled Score. The Record Form provides a "Profile of Abilities" upon which Scaled Scores may be plotted.

Results of the *ITPA*, often presented in profile form, provide information about specific learning abilities. Figure 10 presents a case example of an *ITPA* profile for a student aged 7.6. The scaled scores for this test have a mean of 36 and a standard deviation of 6; thus, this student has scored within

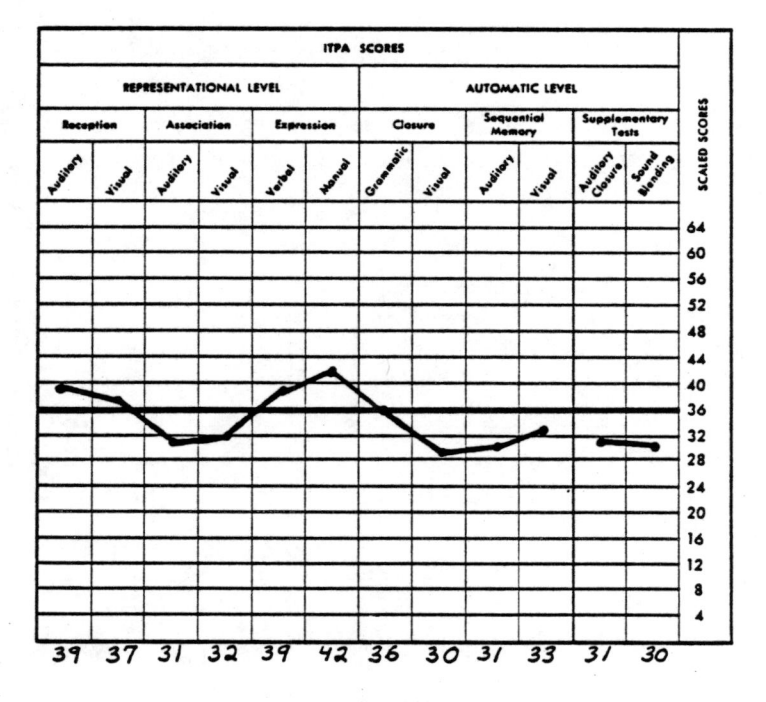

Figure 10. ITPA: Sample Profile. From *Illinois Test of Psycholinguistic Abilities* (Rev. ed.), by S.A. Kirk, J.M. McCarthy, and W.D. Kirk. Urbana: University of Illinois Press. Copyright© 1968 by the Board of Trustees of the University of Illinois. Reprinted by permission.

one standard deviation of the mean of the average population on all subtests.

The results of the *ITPA* should be interpreted with caution. Like many of the other norm-referenced tests, it is perhaps more valuable as an indicator of tendencies in abilities than as a precise measure of specific age level functioning.

Criterion-Referenced Tests

Finally, a student's cumulative records may include results of criterion-referenced-tests (CRT's). Criterion, referenced tests compare a student's performance to some criterion rather than to the performance of other students. While they do not measure whether or not an individual's performance is average for his age, they do provide valuable data about what he or she can and cannot do.

Teachers from a student's earlier years may have constructed their own CRT's or may have used one of several formal inventories available on the commercial market.

The Brigance Diagnostic Inventory of Essential Skills

The *Brigance Diagnostic Inventory of Essential Skills* (Brigance, 1980) is one such CRT. The secondary school inventory covers basic academic and functional skills for independent living. Along with reading, mathematics, and spelling, it probes for the following:

    (1) health and safety, e.g. reads medicine labels
    (2) vocational, e.g. answers job interview questions
    (3) money and finance, e.g. computes interest on loans
    (4) travel and transportation, e.g. figures gas and mileage costs
    (5) food and clothing, e.g. reads food or clothing labels

(6) communication and telephone skills, e.g. uses telephone

Clearly then, there is a great deal of information in cumulative records. Classroom teachers concerned with any aspects of a student's behavior or performance are therefore advised to carefully read through his or her permanent file. Patterns that have not been noted before may exist and may provide the key to the best possible instructional planning for the student with problems in the classroom.

Chapter 5

INFORMAL ASSESSMENTS

UNFORTUNATELY, there is no battery of standardized tests that serves the diagnostic needs of every exceptional learner. Therefore, it is important that concerned teachers supplement the results of formal testing with the use of informal assessment techniques.

Used systematically, informal assessment measures provide invaluable information for instructional planning. Results are highly specific and tend to be directly relevant to classroom performance. In addition, because informal diagnostic procedures are generally used over a span of a whole day or even a whole week, the results are likely to represent truly characteristic behavior. They are, therefore, more reliable than the results of a single, two-hour formal evaluation session, which may be skewed by such factors as the student's anxiety, fatigue, hunger, or emotional response to the tester.

Through informal assessments, it is possible for testers to learn how students respond to a variety of demands, including independent seatwork, group instruction, and the specific requirements and materials of the subject area(s) being evaluated. It is also possible to evaluate whether a student's errors represent random mistakes or a bonafide skill deficit.

There are several types of informal assessment procedures. Teachers may use any one or a combination of several to determine a student's present level of performance and/or to document progress that the student has made.

Observation

Much can be learned through the use of simple observation. A teacher may choose to watch everything a student does for a period of time and then look for patterns; or he may choose a specific behavior, such as the number of times the child gets out of his seat, and note occurrences of only that behavior.

In planning observations, it is important to decide in advance exactly where and when to watch the student and how to record his performance. It is best to plan a variety of time blocks and settings, as students behave quite differently in different situations. The hyperactive child who gets up out of his seat fifteen times during reading class, for example, may sit quietly during the science lesson.

There are numerous checklists, rating scales, and questionnaires available that supplement the use of observation in informal assessment. It is recommended that classroom teachers ask the learning disabilities specialists in their schools for copies of such forms, as they are often helpful in narrowing the scope of diagnostic observation.

Work Sample Analysis

Through work sample analysis a student's performance on a task is scrutinized, to discern areas of strength and weakness. Looking for possible weaknesses, a teacher may use error analysis, describing and categorizing each error made to see if patterns emerge. For example, a teacher may discover that the student consistently substitutes *b* for *d* in oral reading.

Looking for strengths, a teacher may use a response analysis to note the student's correct responses. While there may be many spelling errors in a student's writing assignment, for instance, the child may demonstrate impressive mastery of such basics as grammar and sentence structure.

Criterion-Referenced Tests

Criterion-referenced tests are direct measures of student performance on specific tasks under specific conditions with specific criteria for success. Teachers who wish to use criterion-referenced testing in their classrooms should narrow down specific questions to be answered regarding the student's ability or behavior, e.g. can he recall the months of the year? The next step is to write performance objectives, clearly delineating what the student must do and how well he must do to pass. Objectives include (Mager, 1975) the following:

(1) the desired student behavior, stated in observable terms;
(2) the conditions under which the behavior should occur;
(3) the criteria established for evaluating acceptable performance of this behavior.

An example of a performance objective is, "When asked by the teacher to list the months of the year in order, the student will do so from memory without error within two minutes." If the student passes the criterion-referenced test, he is ready to proceed to the next learning task.

It should be clear to the reader that task analysis is an integral part of this process. The teacher breaks a task down into a sequence of essential subtasks, each of which is then set up as an individual objective for criterion-referenced testing.

Informal Inventories

Finally, there are numerous informal inventories available. Answering more general questions than are addressed in criterion-referenced testing, these inventories help the teacher determine the student's achievement level in relation to the actual curriculum. A teacher might learn, for example, how far a student has progressed in reading. McLoughlin and Lewis suggest the following steps for designing informal inventories (1981, p.176):

(1) Determine the curriculum area in which the student is to be assessed.
(2) Isolate a portion of the curriculum that is appropriate

for the student's age, grade, and skill level.
- (3) Analyze the curriculum in order to separate it into testable and teachable segments. The curriculum may be broken down into sequential steps and/or essential components.
- (4) Write test questions for each testable segment of the curriculum.
- (5) If necessary, reduce the number of test questions so that the test is of manageable length.
- (6) Sequence the test questions either in random order or from easiest to most difficult.

They note that an informal reading inventory would break the reading curriculum into several testable segments, including word recognition, measured by oral reading of both isolated words and paragraphs; and comprehension, measured by oral response to questions about previously read material.

There is no "pass" or "fail" associated with informal inventories. They are used only to estimate the student's present level of academic functioning. The next step is to follow with criterion-referenced testing in suspected problem areas.

The following are suggestions for teachers planning to use informal testing strategies:

- (1) Test in your own classroom, in the same conditions under which the student will be expected to demonstrate skills on a daily basis.
- (2) Test in ten- to twenty-minute periods over the course of several days. Results will be more reliable than if you exhaust the student in one sitting.
- (3) Combine observation with testing. It is the student's *behavior* during testing as much as the product of the task that counts. For example, it is important to note if he is impulsive, highly verbal, hyperactive, etc. during the testing sessions.
- (4) Be careful to separate out environmental conditions, such as noise or drafts, that could interfere with the student's performance.

(5) Do your testing early in the year, so the results will be maximally useful in instructional planning.

It is not possible for teachers to individualize curriculum unless the needs of each student in class are known. As indicated in the last two chapters, diagnostic information is available through numerous sources, including academic, medical, and anecdotal records in the cumulative file; norm-referenced standardized test results; and informal assessment techniques. It is wise to use all three to create the full diagnostic picture of students with learning problems. Only then will it be possible to truly plan for success within the classroom at large.

Chapter 6

USING THIS HANDBOOK

A Case Study

Billy is entering eighth grade. This year he will take a full load of courses, including English, math, science, and social studies. He will attend Resource Room four times per week, as he has for the past four years, to build his basic skills. He has always been a happy-go-lucky boy, motivated despite a very low success record in school.

Although Billy reads quite well, his spelling and writing are extremely weak, (several years below grade level). Auditory discrimination is so deficient that he is likely to misspell almost any word bearing the short vowel sound of *e* or *i*. Other auditory functioning, on the other hand, is adequate.

He forgets how to form letters in cursive, so he prints, but even then he sometimes mixes up *b*'s and *d*'s. His printing is extraordinarily uncontrolled, and between the quality of his handwriting and the level of his spelling, it is very difficult to read any of his papers. His Resource Room teacher reports that when he writes in cursive in her class, both form and content improve, but he fails to use cursive in regular classes because it requires more time than he is generally allotted. His visual memory being quite strong (he is a winner at any form of the game Concentration), she feels he could learn the letters, speed up considerably with practice, and thereby permanently raise the quality of his work.

Billy's math, though weak, has improved. Although he does know the basic number facts, he does not readily recall them. This holds back his progress, for while he is capable of learning higher math concepts, he is bogged down by slow computation.

BILLY could be a student in any school in the country, assigned to any teacher, with or without specialized training. Although inservice courses are becoming increasingly popular, far too few schools have helped their teachers prepare for the trend of mainstreaming children with special needs.

The untrained classroom teacher *can* handle a student with problems of Billy's magnitude by becoming sensitized to the dynamics of learning style, practicing task analysis, and becoming thoroughly familiar with the suggested teaching strategies offered in Chapters 7 to 24.

The case study above provides a fair amount of information on this student. We have a clear picture of some of his strengths and weaknesses. A teacher using this handbook might note the following:

Strengths

Perhaps his greatest strength is his motivation. Although every student wants to succeed, not everyone shares Billy's willingness to work for success.

(1) Billy reads well. This represents a distinct and valuable channel through which new information may be processed.

(2) He also has strong visual and auditory memory, so there seems to be little problem with reception of new knowledge.

Weaknesses

Billy's greatest weakness is in written *expression.*

(1) His slowness in cursive writing and his tendency to misform letters suggests a VISUAL-MOTOR problem.

(2) His AUDITORY DISCRIMINATION problem interrupts his learning and interferes with the quality of his written work.

(3) His WEAK AUTOMATIZATION SKILLS have hampered his math progress and have kept him from speeding up his writing.

Billy's classroom teachers should capitalize on his strengths, encouraging reading and positively reinforcing his strong motivation. To address his weaknesses, his teachers could use some of the teaching strategies suggested in the following chapters under:

    Visual-motor deficits: pages 86-87
    Auditory discrimination problems: pages 68-70
    Weak automatization skills: pages 65-67

Although the strategy lists have been compiled from a variety of sources, they do not represent a finite collection of approaches. Each student is unique and, therefore, so are his needs. Teachers are encouraged to read the suggestions listed, adjusting and expanding them to meet the particular special needs of the students in their classes.

Section II
Areas of Special Needs

Chapter 7

DISTRACTIBILITY

DEFINITION OF DISTRACTIBILITY: Limited ability to "tune out" extraneous stimuli; supersensitivity to both internal and external stimuli

Observable Behaviors

- The child is apt to have particular problems paying attention when there are extraneous environmental stimuli present. Noises from the gym, cafeteria or outside playing field; interesting book covers or attractive classmates; movements of other students to the pencil sharpener and around the room; all represent signals for distraction.
- He may experience quick shifts in interest and little capacity for sustained effort. This student begins a project with good intentions but often loses interest and may fail to carry the task to completion.
- He may have difficulty structuring goals, planning ahead, and anticipating consequences. He is likely to struggle when given long-term assignments, easily slipping off task and often leaving the work to the last minute before the actual due date.
- He may lose interest in abstract materials. He seems to learn best when the curriculum provides for the use of concrete materials that offer sensory stimulation.
- He may have difficulty automatizing repetitive functions such as assembly hall procedures or cafeteria routines.
- He may be more than normally distracted by physiological distress (pain, hunger, fatigue) and, therefore, less attentive to instruction just prior to lunch or late in the afternoon.
- He may have weak recall skills, due to problems screening distractions when information is being offered.

Teaching Strategies

- Seat the student where he is least likely to be distracted by either other students in the room or by activities outside of the room. Avoid placing him by the windows, where his attention might easily be drawn to noises outside on the playground, or by the door, where he might get caught up in goings-on in the corridor. The front row may be an appropriate seating area, or you may choose to provide the student with a study carrel.
- Reduce potentially distracting visual variables, such as old notes left on the blackboard.
- Try to anticipate and avoid other situations that contribute to distractible behavior, such as consistent speaking out by several people at once during classroom discussions.
- Try to remember that the distractible child is rarely successful in attending to announcements made during the class or during between-class transitions.
- Announce assignments and other news items *before* the bell has rung to mark the end of class.
- Through careful observation, it is possible to determine the student's current attention span. Try to build on it: start by providing assignments that fit within his natural limits; then gradually lengthen demands by five minute increments. Using a cooking timer to indicate the passage of specific periods can be very helpful to students.
- Provide firm rules, clearly stating the consequences of breaking them.
- Recognize and reinforce socially acceptable behavior wherever possible. For example, praise the student for having continued to attend to the teacher's lecture when a screaming fire engine drove by during social studies class.
- Provide outlets for the student's restlessness. Reward attentive behavior by allowing him to carry messages to the main office or to work on a puzzle for three minutes between activities. Again, a kitchen timer may be used to indicate

when the reward period is over.
- Include periods of reduced sensory stimulation in the day's schedule. Quiet moments in a section of the room that is visually uncluttered can be used for listening to music or to a story read aloud.

Chapter 8

IMPULSIVITY

DEFINITION OF IMPULSIVITY: The impulsive child characteristically makes quick erroneous decisions. He reacts immediately, as if by reflex.

Observable Behaviors

- The child is unable to readily delay gratification of needs or desires. He cannot handle waiting and frequently pouts or acts out when asked to wait his turn.
- The child may demonstrate what may appear to be bizarre behavior. He may frequently interrupt others, may blurt out an answer in the middle of a classmate's response, may rise up out of his seat and wander aimlessly around the room in the middle of a lecture period. His difficulty conforming to specified behavioral limits is more likely due to a lack of internal controls, however, than to a fundamental oddness in personality.
- He may touch and handle inappropriate objects within his environment. He is the first to "explore" the bunson burner, the shop machinery, or the new computer without permission. Because he does not stop to consider consequences, he often places himself and others in potentially dangerous situations.
- He may respond too quickly on an emotional level. Failing to carefully think things through, he responds by impulse in sensitive situations. He may injure or insult someone as a result of a quick reaction and then immediately feel sorry for his response. The impulsive child is often genuinely surprised by what he has just done.

Impulsivity

Teaching Strategies

- Help the child inhibit impulses. Teach him that many different responses may be viable and that all available alternatives must be considered prior to responding. Do not reinforce impulsive actions. For example, it is best to ignore him when he shouts out an answer without raising his hand.
- Eliminate potential distractions, such as extra materials on the child's desk. Have him put away any extra books or papers that are not being used during his period in your class. Provide a study carrel, if possible, for individual periods.
- Provide firm rules, clearly stating the consequences of breaking them. You may want to insist that the student be quiet when others are speaking and that he raise his hand rather than speaking out in class. Or you may want to suggest that he count to five and think again before he impulsively answers a question.
- Provide highly structured routines, such as specific time periods during which the child must be seated at this desk. Assign one task daily to which he *must* attend if he is to continue with the rest of the class. Allow a structured five to ten minute period during which the student may count on receiving your undivided attention each day.
- Engineer situations requiring progressively longer waiting periods prior to gratification. Teach the student how to wait by withholding rewards, i.e. praise or privileges, a little longer every day.
- Recognize and reinforce socially acceptable behavior whenever possible. Praise him for raising his hand to answer questions during math period, and congratulate him for thinking through his responses prior to offering them in class.

Chapter 9

HYPERACTIVITY

DEFINITION OF HYPERACTIVITY: persistent, heightened, and sustained activity levels that are situationally and socially appropriate

Observable Behaviors

- The child may exhibit greater motor activity than others in his peer group. It is very difficult for him to remain in his seat, and he is constantly in motion, tapping his pencil, jiggling his knees, or pacing the aisles. His actions often seem to be involuntary, as he is frequently restless even when intensely interested in the subject being presented.
- He may have good intentions. He may readily start on an assignment but be defeated by a plethora of energy and a lack of self-control. With little capacity for sustained effort, he rarely completes his work. Ultimately, his motivation diminishes considerably, along with his self-concept as a learner.
- He may be a weak automatizer, rarely sustaining attention long enough to really learn the multiplication tables, his locker combination, or his daily schedule of classes.
- He may demonstrate wide fluctuations of performance in the classroom, with work ranging from excellent to unacceptable in quality. Because of this inconsistent learning pattern, he acquires less information and remains at a lower skills level than others of his intellectual ability. Consequently, he generally scores poorly on objective tests of school achievement.
- He may exhibit various weaknesses in the fine motor area. Because he cannot be bothered attending to the fine details of handwriting, he is likely to write illegibly. For the same

reasons, he probably does not do well in the graphic arts.
- He may be extremely untidy. Notebook, desks and lockers are stuffed with papers and books that he cannot stand still long enough to organize. His shirt is often untucked, his shoelaces untied.
- He may be rejected by friends, particularly as he grows older, as his peers develop attention spans for more sedentary hobbies, such as model-making. Repeated experiences of his own disruptive behavior causing peer rejection further lead to development of low self-image.

Teaching Strategies

- Teach the student to sit still for gradually lengthening periods of time. Reward him with praise after five minutes of self-control. Later, extend a challenge for him to sit quietly for ten minutes. Praise him when he accomplishes this. Firmly remind him, if he should begin to fail, that he is trying to be controlled. Between periods of calm, allow him to unleash his energy in some "legal" pursuit, such as running an errand or erasing the blackboard.
- Help him learn to monitor his behavior on the basis of cues from the environment. Offer a private personal cue, a raised eyebrow or a tug at your ear, that will tell the child when he is going too far. Getting him to watch the teacher's cue is a fine first step toward eventual self-monitoring.
- Provide firm rules with clear consequences for failure to comply with them. Provide immediate specific verbal reinforcement when he follows through, e.g. "You watched Bobby all the way through his talk on whales. That's good paying-attention." Provide firm, gentle, consistent pressure toward gradually expanding his responsibility for behaving according to the rules of the school.
- Help him learn to plan ahead, to structure goals and anticipate consequences. If he is assigned to read a book, help him chart out how many pages will have to be read each

night in order to finish by the due date. Discuss the possible consequences of not following through.
- Help the student with organization. Give him tips on his note-taking and see that he gets important information down in a reasonably organized format. Monitor his notebook, checking that papers are being "filed" by subject matter and that homework is being recorded and completed as assigned. Periodically check his desk or locker for general neatness and for overdue library books.

Chapter 10

PERSEVERATION

DEFINITION OF PERSEVERATION: tendency for a specific act, behavior, or attitude to continue in operation when it is no longer appropriate to the situation at hand

Observable Behaviors

- The child may prolong reactions. Almost any behavior, attitude, or emotion may be perseverated. A child may continue laughing at a joke or crying over an incident long beyond a reasonable period of time.
- He may bring up the same topics of conversation over and over again with every person he meets.
- He may produce drawings with the same figure or part of a figure drawn repeatedly. If he is young, he may draw circles again and again; if he is older, he may continue a line beyond the border of the paper.
- He may use the same response again and again when answering a variety of questions. Or he may ask the same question ad nauseum.
- He may have difficulty shifting behaviors or changing attitudes. He is likely to be perceived as stubborn.
- He may have difficulty adjusting to new activities. This student experiences problems during between-class transitions and may resist the changes in schedule that frequently occur in school settings during any one academic year.

Teaching Strategies

- Design instructional activities that demand variation in response. Emphasize the need for varieties of answers, and reinforce the student for shifting appropriately from thought

to thought.
- Vary the materials by which information is presented. Use audio-visual equipment, manipulatives, dramatic play and other methods to avoid the routines that foster perseveration.
- If possible, change classroom variables such as seating locations as the year progresses. This, too, breaks routinization and helps the perseverative child learn how to adapt to new situations.
- Provide either verbal or nonverbal cues to interrupt the perseverative behavior. Gently calling out the child's name or touching him on the shoulder can be very helpful.

Chapter 11

WEAK AUTOMATIZATION

DEFINITION OF WEAK AUTOMATIZATION: great difficulty making repetitive, routine aspects of a task become automatic habits that require little conscious awareness or attention.

Observable Behaviors

- The child may approach each task as if it were a new experience, regardless of the amount of his past experience with the same or similar tasks. He may learn the 8s multiplication table one day and have lost it by the next math class. Thus, he may need to rely upon finger counting or wild calculations to arrive at the fact that 3 × 8 equals 24.
- He may suffer from gaps in his knowledge due to weak automatization. Because he often cannot readily recite the alphabet, he has considerable difficulty using telephone books, encyclopedias, and dictionaries. Because he may be unable to remember the full sequence of the months and holidays in a year, he is likely to feel lost when a teacher assigns a project due "just before Easter vacation."
- He may have impaired handwriting skills. He is likely to have difficulty recalling how the letters are formed and how they are linked in script. His handwriting is typically a mishmash of upper case and lower case letters, half written and half printed.
- He may perform poorly in situations requiring precision and speed. Because of this, he scores low on timed tests.
- He may have difficulty learning routines. He is likely to forget such things as the location of his assigned locker and the sequence of opening exercises in homeroom each morning.

- He may have poor rote and/or sequential memory. He does not memorize frequently used phone numbers and often cannot remember more than a few words of familiar songs. In addition, despite considerable drill in class, he often cannot master his spelling list.
- He may have various difficulties with spoken language. He may find it difficult to choose the appropriate tense of verbs or the correct plural forms or the accurate pronounciation of fairly common words.
- He may struggle with time and space concepts. It is likely that he cannot read the time accurately from nondigital clockfaces; that even in March he still loses his way when going from math to gym class; that he distorts the body when asked to draw a figure in art class.

Teaching Strategies

- Alert the student when you are reviewing or generalizing concepts that have been previously presented in class. Help him become aware that information is not always being newly introduced and that the review process is crucial to learning.
- Allow extra time for the student to learn the rules of a game or for completion of time-limited tests requiring automatization skills.
- Remind the student where he has been sitting, when he forgets. Help him devise a method of remembering the location of his locker and classes. Suggest that he write down phone numbers and that he keep them in a safe spot.
- Help him with time-space concepts. Help him learn to read the nondigital clock with full accuracy and to remember the months of the year in order. In art or science class, show him how the body is formed and how the various parts make the whole.
- Keep gently drilling those sequences and facts that are within the child's realm of possible learning. It is likely that

he *can* learn to alphabetize and multiply if the material is presented enough times in enough ways, and with sufficient review. Be careful, however, not to badger the student with excessive drilling. Some students with persistent automatization difficulties may become discouraged and frustrated at their failure to master the math facts; they would be better served by being taught to use a calculator or math chart than by continuing to suffer through repeated multiplication drills.
- Provide as many reviews of specific information as necessary without displays of impatience or antagonism toward the student. He will be less easily frustrated, less embarrassed by his weakness in automatization, and will more readily master the learning tasks at hand.

Chapter 12

INADEQUATE AUDITORY DISCRIMINATION

DEFINITION OF INADEQUATE AUDITORY DISCRIMINATION: inability to interpret or organize the sensory data received through the ears.

Observable Behaviors

- The child may have trouble distinguishing between individual sounds in spoken language. He may have trouble differentiating between such sounds as *sh* and *ch* or *th* and *ph*. Consequently, because it is impossible to properly mimic a sound that has been incorrectly heard, he may demonstrate inaccuracies in pronunciation of new vocabulary or foreign words, making it likely that he will perform poorly in foreign language classes or in courses requiring the oral use of new terms.
- He may be unable to recognize differences between whole words that may be similar in sound, such as *pen* and *pin*, *shop* and *chop*. This problem affects both pronunciation and writing.
- He may have spelling problems that reflect the above auditory confusions. He may know the names but not the sounds of letters, or he may know the sounds but be unable to blend them into words. Thus, he is likely to choose the wrong vowels and blends in his spelling. Or he may omit vowels altogether from words, e.g. *wrm* for *warm*; may leave off the second consonant in blends, e.g. *rus* for *rust*; or frequently eliminate suffixes in words.
- He may fail at games requiring rhyming and rhythm.
- He may have difficulty with pitch, frequency, and intensity.
- He is likely to be a weak music student, and because he

often speaks in a monotone or unnatural pitch, he may have difficulty portraying moods and personality in a drama class.

Teaching Strategies

- Face the child and speak slowly and distinctly. Encourage him to look at you and read your lips when you speak. Seat the student in a central position, near the front of the room, if that is the most appropriate location for maximum view of speakers' faces.
- Provide visual reinforcement as often as possible when you speak to the class: provide an outline of your lectures; use graphs and tables to reinforce concepts; note all announced assignments on the blackboard, in a consistent predesignated boxed-in homework area.
- Divide longer orally assigned tasks into shorter ones, according to the principles of task analysis. By doing this, you offer the student a chance to digest each part separately and to succeed many times in the completion of one assignment. As the student improves in taking oral directions, gradually increase your expectations and demands on his ability.
- As much as possible, limit outside noises that would lead the student to make faulty discriminations between sounds in class. If noises persist, it may be helpful to allow him to use a tape cassette to record class lectures and discussions. While the student should be encouraged to take notes on what he hears, he may relax if he knows that the tape recorder will catch any subtleties of language or informational details that he might miss.
- Provide practice in noticing, describing, and comparing details. Have the student listen carefully to two sounds, two sentences, or even two paragraphs and discuss any similarities and differences he may have discerned.
- Provide extra explanation and demonstration in your instructional curriculum. Students with auditory problems often benefit enormously from supplementary visual work,

which helps them grasp the material presented orally.
- Check frequently that the student is not erring due to misreceipt of information. This may be done by having him periodically summarize important details from your lectures.
- Write out new vocabulary and technical terms on the blackboard so that the student may visualize them. If necessary, provide a written glossary for him.

Chapter 13

WEAK AUDITORY FIGURE-GROUND DISCRIMINATION

DEFINITION OF WEAK AUDITORY FIGURE-GROUND DISCRIMINATION: the inability to pick out necessary and relevant sounds from extraneous background noises

Observable Behaviors

- The child may be easily distracted by extraneous noises such as loud discussions in the class next door or fire engines going by in the traffic outside. He may also be distracted by far more subtle noises, such as the hum of the fluorescent lighting overhead or of the heating system blower at the back of the room or of the school's 16mm film projector.
- He may function poorly in an open education environment, where there are many noise-producing activities happening at one time within the classroom itself.
- He may display little capacity for concentration on pure auditory stimulation, such as lectures or language lab tapes. Because he cannot sustain attention to the primary auditory stimulus at hand, the student often pursues inappropriate activities during classtime. Thus, either his withdrawal or his interruption of others' worktime represents behavior problems that often interfere with the goings-on in class.
- He may seem to have poor auditory memory. Because other noises have kept him from attending, he is often unable to recall recently presented auditory experiences.
- He may tune out, particularly in a noisy environment. Since he cannot easily tune in to any one sound, he stops listening altogether as a defense against "auditory overload."

Teaching Strategies

- Speak carefully, with clear articulation, facing the student.
- Seat him appropriately in the classroom away from sources of potential distractions such as open windows, noisy heat blowers, or other talkative children. Be sure that he is seated as far as possible from the hum of audiovisual equipment when it is in use.
- Following oral presentations or lecture-type classes, ask several questions on the content covered to check that the student has tuned in to the primary stimulus.
- Provide the child with quiet space for times when classroom noises are clearly distracting him. Earphones or wax ear stopples may be used to screen out distractions, particularly during test periods. Wax stopples are very helpful and are available inexpensively in most drugstores; however, it is important to check with the school nurse before suggesting that a student insert any foreign object into the ear cavity.
- Make sure all assignments are written on the blackboard so that the student will not be penalized for being unable to attend when homework is announced. Avoid the traditional pattern of trying to shout the evening's assignment at the end of class, when the noise of closing books, shifting papers, and clicking notebooks is at its peak. Announcing assignments well before the period ends allows students the time to ask any necessary clarifying questions and to accurately copy the homework from the board into their assignment notebooks.
- Provide visual reinforcement as often as possible, such as outlines, graphs, and tables, to help the student sustain attention to material presented orally in class.

Chapter 14

AUDITORY MEMORY DEFICITS

DEFINITION OF AUDITORY MEMORY DEFICITS: inability to store and retrieve upon demand previously experienced auditory perceptions, particularly once the original sound is no longer present

Observable Behaviors

- The child is apt to frequently ask to have oral directions repeated. While he may remember some elements of what was said, he may be unable to recall them all. Or he may be unable to recall the *sequence* of the directions, leading him, for example, to mix the chemicals in science class in the wrong order.
- He may have difficulty maintaining interest during orally presented lessons. He cannot recall the details of what he hears and, therefore, may be unable to understand a point as it is being developed over the course of a forty-minute lecture class.
- He may have trouble memorizing common sequences, such as the alphabet or months of the year. Because he has great difficulty repeating sequences, he is likely to have problems in alphabetizing, remembering phone numbers, or recalling the zip code of his home address.
- He may forget songs, poems, or common jingles. This is the child who will not be able to use "30 days hath September . . . " to remember the number of days in March or November. And this is the child who will often transpose or omit words when asked to memorize a few lines of poetry.
- He may exhibit mild speech irregularities, as he forgets the correct pronunciation of certain words. Because he cannot

easily remember the sequence of sounds, he will often transpose the syllables in polysyllabic words such as *aluminum* or *synonym*.
- He may have difficulty recalling new vocabulary words that have been orally presented and explained in class.

Teaching Strategies

- Provide visual clues and reinforcements whenever possible in lecture classes. Demonstrations, outlines, charts, diagrams, and pictures are invaluable in this capacity. Supplement oral instructions with written directions, providing ample time for the student to copy them into his notebook.
- Very gradually help the student learn to take directions without visual clues. Give him very short, one-concept directions at first, making sure he has grasped what is expected before moving on to the next step. Slowly lengthen oral directions, and broaden your demands.
- Give the student extra time to respond to oral questions. It may take him a little longer to process the inquiry and organize an answer. Be patient.
- Have the student look at you when you speak. By encouraging him to pay particular attention to your lips and gestures, you are teaching him a compensatory practice which takes advantage of visual clues to the oral message being conveyed.
- Teach the student that another way to compensate for his auditory memory weakness is to write down important information such as names, phone numbers, addresses, and assignments as they are orally presented to him. He may wish to carry a small notepad with him at all times to record such information.
- Present the key points of a lecture at the beginning of your talk; summarize them again at the end.
- Check that the student has attended to and retained orally presented material by periodically having him repeat key

points of the information covered.
- Encourage the student to visualize what he hears, to create a mental picture that will help him retain the information at hand. Teach him how to use acronyms to help him recall sequences, i.e. HOMES for the Great Lakes.
- Be careful not to overload the student with listening tasks. Provide a balance of visual and auditory stimuli in your classroom teaching.

Chapter 15

WEAK VISUAL DISCRIMINATION

D<small>EFINITION OF</small> W<small>EAK</small> V<small>ISUAL</small> D<small>ISCRIMINATION</small>: inability to visually distinguish one object from another

Observable Behaviors

- The child is apt to reverse letters and numbers. He may print a *b* as a *d*, or a *6* as a *9*. Or he may invert the order of numbers and letters, reading or writing *36* as *63* or the word *was* as *saw*.
- He may tilt his head "to see better." Many people with visual discrimination problems rotate an item, seeing a square as a diamond, for example. Sometimes they will tilt the whole head to compensate for this misreceived information.
- He may have difficulty with depth perception and size discrimination. The child who always fails at bean-bags or horseshoes, the student who fails to notice that Russia is larger than Poland, has difficulties in this area.
- He may have difficulty discriminating between look-alike words such as *pen — pin*. He may have trouble distinguishing between words with similar shapes, such as *boy — dog*. Or he may find it difficult to discriminate between *objects* with similar shapes, such as beakers and graduated cylinders in science class.
- He may have difficulty with different types of script. He may recognize a particular sight word in print but not be able to read it in cursive. Or he may lose the ability to read it when it is presented in italics. Similarly, he may be inconsistent in recognition of words or pictures in various contexts.
- He may derive less enjoyment than others from pictures, since "looking" (as contrasted to "seeing") is a problem for him.

- He may have difficulty copying. Since he has trouble discriminating the details of shapes and words, he is apt to transfer faulty information onto his paper. He is particularly frustrated when required to copy from the blackboard, as the change in plane from board to desk complicates the task considerably.
- He may have difficulty comparing and contrasting newly seen items due to his inability to note finer details.

Teaching Strategies

- Be sure mimeographed papers are fully legible. Avoid giving out streaked sheets or any that are blurred by copying on both sides.
- If the master is homemade, include enough blank space to provide visual relief from line after line of sentences. It often helps to alternate between double and single spacing. Pictures and diagrams not only offer further explanation but also tend to make a page more psychologically approachable by breaking up the text.
- Allow the student to sit where he can see the board comfortably. Point out details of visual items so that he might mentally register them for later recall. Help him compare visual items until he is able to do this on his own. Ask him to look carefully at the words *pen — pin*, for example, and tell you how they are alike and different. Check his notebook frequently to see that he is copying information correctly from the board or from his reading.
- Have the student verbalize written directions to check that he understands what he is to do. By doing this, you will detect early enough any errors in reading that would have him doing the assignment incorrectly.
- Point out evidence of reversals, and help him think of tricks to avoid making them again. For example, it is easier to remember how to distinguish *b* and *d* if one remembers the configuration of the word *bed*.

- Help the student enjoy looking at pictures. Challenge him to observe details and quiz him orally to make a game of it. Then change positions, allowing him to pick the details and quiz you. Such games provide sound remedial activity in a very motivating format.
- Help him learn size discrimination in a similar fashion, through games and exercises. Ask him to discriminate from across the room which of two beakers contains more liquid; then ask him to measure. Ask him to discern from his seat which of two geometric shapes drawn on the board is smaller; then have him check his answer by measuring. With enough practice of this sort, his ability to estimate and discriminate size differences will improve.
- If you notice that a student is exhibiting symptoms suggesting problems of depth perception (tossing a ball far short of the target, bumping into desks, etc.) be sure to refer him to a physician for a proper ophthalmological examination as soon as possible.

Chapter 16

WEAK VISUAL FIGURE-GROUND DISCRIMINATION

DEFINITION OF WEAK VISUAL FIGURE-GROUND DISCRIMINATION: inability to pull out and focus on one figure from a visual background

Observable Behaviors

- The child is apt to have difficulty locating the word he is seeking on a dictionary page or the phone number he is pursuing in the phone book.
- He may look flustered when the math teacher directs the class to focus on example number sixteen on a worksheet of twenty-five items. He cannot easily telescope in on one item on a crowded page.
- He may have great difficulty finding his place again in the social studies chapter or English poem after the teacher has stopped for a few minutes' discussion.
- He may have trouble picking out specific locations from a large area map. He struggles to find Paris in a map of Europe and cannot easily find Australia on a globe.
- He may struggle with microscope work, such as finding the specific cells within tissue samples. He also has difficulty with general lab tasks, such as focussing on one organ in a dissected frog's chest cavity.
- He may accidentally skip sections of a test or omit parts of an assignment. If he looks up from the paper momentarily to check the time, he may return to another section of the page and never notice his error.
- He may fail to accurately copy notes from a section of the blackboard when the rest of its surface is still filled with old

information and extraneous scribblings.
- He may have difficulty reading some charts and diagrams. This is due to problems distinguishing the parts of a whole.

Teaching Strategies

- Try not to present too much information on one page of reading material. Overly crowded papers tend to confuse and frighten students.
- It is often helpful to use frequent indentations, double spacing, and boxes around key words to provide visual clues for the reader with figure-ground difficulties.
- Structure the space on math worksheets as much as possible. Examples should be lined up with vertical and horizontal lines, creating boxes that clearly delineate the appropriate work area.
- Structure the work space on other mimeographed assignments as well. Clearly note *how large* the assigned diagram should be or *where* the answers to the poetry questions should be written.
- Try not to mimeograph on both sides of a sheet of paper. The ink tends to bleed through, often making the entire paper virtually illegible. This common problem creates difficulties for all but is particularly frustrating to the student suffering from poor visual figure-ground skills.
- Encourage the student to use his finger or a marker to keep his place when he is reading. Although most children have been *forbidden* to do this in the past, they should know that finger tracking will improve their performance as long as they do not revert to word-by-word reading. Some students may prefer to use a large index card or paper cut with a "window" large enough to permit viewing of only the required section of work.
- Help the student see part-whole relationships through outlining, coloring and cross-hatching. For example, provide maps with key countries emphasized by color and black

outlines, or graphs with key components cross-hatched.
- Have the student remove all but the material with which he is working from his desk. If he is trying to focus on one item at a time in a book, he will only be distracted by the presence of extra notebooks and rulers on the work surface before him.
- Offer remedial exercises, such as sorting one kind of plastic molecule from a box of many for science; tracing one shape on a sheet bearing many overlapping shapes for geometry; or cutting out specific countries from a map of Europe for Social Studies.
- Keep the blackboard erased of all but pertinent visual stimuli. To help students distinguish a key item from the rest of the writing on the board, use brackets, circles, or underlinings with colored chalk for visual emphasis. Delineate one special boxed-in section of the blackboard as the only area on which homework assignments will be written. Students will benefit greatly from this consistency.

Chapter 17

VISUAL MEMORY DEFICITS

DEFINITION OF VISUAL MEMORY DEFICITS: inability to store and retrieve upon demand previously perceived stimuli

Observable Behaviors

- The child is apt to be unable to recall how to form all the letters in handwriting. He may mix up capitals and small letters in printing, e.g. *cAt*, or he may randomly insert printed letters when writing in cursive.
- He may have difficulty recalling written sequences. He struggles with math tables and alphabetical lists and is less likely than others to grasp sequences of events taught through time lines. He has trouble committing instrumental pieces to memory from sheet music.
- He may be inconsistent in remembering sight words he reads. For example, he may be able to read the word *thought* correctly one day and completely fail to recognize it the next.
- He may have similar difficulty with spelling sight words. He may learn to spell an irregular word such as *said* during one class and then proceed to misspell it during the next, or he may write the correct letters but in the wrong sequence, spelling *said* as *siad*.
- He may have trouble reproducing other visual objects or symbols such as jigsaw puzzles or codes. He may be able to recognize a symbol when given a model but be unable to recall it on his own when the model is no longer present.
- He may have limited ability to think in terms of visual concepts. He cannot easily *revisualize* or conjure up images from memory. Therefore, if he has not cognitively mastered the

fact that X chemical added to Y will produce Z, he will not be able to answer a related science question, as many others do, by simply picturing how the teacher performed the experiment earlier in class.
- He may have similar difficulty *visualizing* information. If given a word problem, delivered orally by his math teacher, he is not likely to be able to compute the problem through mental imagery. He may react emotionally when asked to do an example "in his head."
- He may misplace his belongings on a regular basis. He puts them down and cannot recall where they were left. He cannot visually "return to the scene" and retrace his steps to retrieve the lost articles. He often becomes spatially confused, forgetting how to position his work on a sheet of paper or the difference between *up — down, left — right* and other directionality concepts.
- He may be unable to sustain interest or attention during visually presented lessons. Because he often cannot remember what he sees, he may forget crucial steps of a science demonstration, or in a social studies film, he may forget earlier scenes and be unable to follow later plot developments.

Teaching Strategies

- Remember that this student's comprehension will be better with oral than visual presentations. Conduct whole-class and small-group discussions as often as possible to review the content of visually presented materials.
- Provide opportunities for the student to read material aloud, either quietly to himself or aloud to others. The added auditory component will help him retain the information being read.
- Build up a tape cassette library of reading materials commonly used in your class, and allow the student to read along with the recorded version of any assignment. Again,

this auditory reinforcement of the visual material will enhance long-term retention of the information covered.
- Explain the value of auditory reinforcement and encourage the student to provide himself with auditory stimuli as often as possible by talking about reading material to friends and family or by reciting information aloud to himself.
- Play memory games. *Concentration* is a marvelous teaching device that can be tailored to any subject area. A match could be made in English class by picking a book title card and its appropriate author card; in science, a chemical and its formula; in math, equations and their answers; in social studies, countries and their capitals. The possibilities are limitless.
- Teach the student to use mnemonic devices such as acronyms, rhymes, and songs to help him visualize and internalize information he reads.
- Encourage the student to develop a system for storing his personal equipment. If he knows that it is his rule to always put his pencil in a notebook pouch, he will not be likely to panic when asked to pull out a writing utensil in class. Likewise for homework: if he has one special section in his notebook for completed homework, he is less apt to experience those frantic searches we have all witnessed in the past.
- Further encourage visual organization by writing out a schedule of the class routines. It is also helpful to provide a written timeline for long-term assignments.
- Allow the student to trace over geometric shapes and other important visual patterns. This movement offers kinesthetic reinforcement that will help visual memory.
- Have the student read the examples aloud as he uses math flashcards. This, again, provides auditory reinforcement of the visual stimulus. Some students learn new spelling words more easily this way too, by saying the letters as they write them.
- Build memory and encourage observation by having the

student carefully examine a picture relevant to your material for one minute, then answer questions on the content after the picture has been removed. Do the same thing with short filmstrips.
- Reteach items of information as often as possible, varying your approach a little each time.
- Maximize the student's potential for success by providing a balance of visual and auditory stimuli in your teaching. Offer outlines on the blackboard when conducting discussion sessions; offer discussion of the content when the class is expected to have covered independent reading materials.

Chapter 18

VISUAL-MOTOR DEFICITS

DEFINITION OF VISUAL-MOTOR DEFICITS: inability to coordinate vision with the movements of the body or parts of the body.

Observable Behaviors

- The child is apt to exhibit poor eye-hand coordination. If he has a fine motor deficit, he may have uncontrolled handwriting and much difficulty in activities such as cutting, sewing, drawing and copying. Frequently this student is able to see his mistakes and is frustrated by his inability to either translate what is seen onto the page or to correct the errors that he makes.
- He may be rather clumsy in his movements. If he has a gross motor deficit, he is likely to break things or run into things simply because he is unable to coordinate his eyes and limbs.

Teaching Strategies

- Have a model alphabet posted in the classroom for students who may forget how some of the more complex letters are formed. Older students may wish to have a mimeographed sample to store in their notebooks, for a somewhat more discreet reference when necessary.
- Encourage the student to use only lined paper for writing. In this way he will avoid the "bending sentences" that often characterize the essay on unruled plain white paper.
- Suggest that the child skip lines when writing compositions. This practice allows plenty of room for erasures and revisions of rough drafts and provides for easier deciphering by

the reader.
- Try to minimize the student's tension level by varying the writing requirements assigned to him. Offer multiple choice items, matching exercises, or oral quizzes as a balance to essay assignments.
- If the student must take a written essay exam with the rest of the class, it will relieve some of the pressure if he can be offered extra time after school to complete the test at his own pace.
- Sometimes it may be helpful to allow the child to tape-record his answers to test questions. This is not desirable as a general practice, however, as it removes all possibilities of the student's learning to cope with writing requirements. It is preferable to provide the additional work time necessary for the student to compensate for his eye-hand coordination difficulties or to have him write his essay answers in outline form.
- Encourage the student to use cursive writing whenever possible. The flowing motion of cursive is far easier to master than the staccato movement of manuscript. Typing, though difficult, is another alternative, which again requires less complex fine motor coordination than printing.
- Avoid exposing him to potentially humiliating competition. While it is important that he have an opportunity to join the class in its softball game, the clumsy child may prefer to be the scorekeeper than to consistently miss the ball when he is up at bat. To ensure greater success in future activities of this sort, however, this student should be provided with remedial batting practice either privately after school or in adaptive physical education classes.
- Encourage participation in noncompetitive activities such as ball catching and throwing, nail pounding, and sewing. Cooking is another excellent pasttime, with measuring, peeling, and pouring all requiring eye-hand coordination, and with a delicious built-in reinforcement at the end!

Chapter 19

DIFFICULTIES WITH VISUAL-SPATIAL RELATIONSHIPS

DEFINITION OF DIFFICULTIES WITH VISUAL-SPATIAL RELATIONSHIPS: inability to relate oneself to space and subsequent inability to relate sets of objects in space to each other.

Observable Behaviors

- The child is apt to have handwriting problems:
  - His letters are often poorly organized on the paper, either spaced too far apart or too tightly crowded together. Spacing between words and sentences also tends to be inappropriate.
  - The student may have trouble consistently writing on the lines when using standard notebook paper.
  - His writing may be riddled with inconsistencies in letter size. He may print a small *e*, for example, that is twice the size of his capital *D*.
- He may have difficulties organizing his work on a sheet of paper. He poorly estimates the amount of space needed to write his full name in the upper right hand corner of the page and the amount of room that is needed to draw a diagram of his science experiment.
- He may make unnecessary math errors when his spatial alignments are off in computation examples.
- He may run beyond the work area limits of a particular math item, with calculations overlapping the example appearing below it on the page.
- He may become easily disoriented in space. He easily loses his way in situations where it is necessary to take alternate routes from those normally taken. He may, for example,

become confused when he has to enter school through a side door instead of the central entrance to which he is accustomed. It is harder for him to "catch his bearings" than it is for most people.
- He may struggle with directionality concepts. He often confuses *left* and *right* and *north—south—east—west*. Because of these confusions and an inability to grasp estimations of distance, he has much trouble with map work.
- He may experience difficulty when doing outline work. He cannot remember when to indent or where to place the main ideas in relation to supporting details.
- He may become anxious when asked to draw microscope sketches or scaled map work. He is aware that he will have trouble representing the image with spatial accuracy.

Teaching Strategies

- To help the student keep his handwriting within the lines, provide a writing template, a heavy cardboard sheet the same size as his paper. The cardboard will help to alert him to the spatial limits appropriate for written work.
- Teach the student that when writing a paper, his name should be no longer than one or two forefingers in length in the upper right hand corner of the sheet.
- Help the student differentiate between left and right. One way to do this is to provide a dimestore ring to always be worn on the right hand. Another way is to teach the child that by curling his fingers and extending the thumb and forefinger of the left hand, he can create the letter *L*. "*L* = left" is an easy mnemonic device.
- Provide opportunities for the student to practice orienting himself in space. Structure simple map work, treasure hunts, and errands to unfamiliar areas in school in such a way that he cannot fail. Gradually increase the demands made on his spatial orientation.
- Help him learn to estimate distances and measurements.

Again, provide simple, guided exercises that ensure success. Have him guess the distances from his desk to the door or to the blackboard and then measure them. Have him look carefully at maps. Help him see that France and Germany are juxtaposed and approximately equal in size on a map of Europe, and contrast these with the size and dimensions of Russia-Poland or Norway-Sweden.
- Be patient with the student's drawings and diagrams. Try to help him depict images with spatial accuracy. Graph paper may be useful, as it provides a framework in which the student may use grids to draw to scale. Note his progress and positively reinforce his efforts.

Chapter 20

CONCEPTUALIZATION DIFFICULTIES

Definition of Conceptualization Difficulties: a disturbance in the ability to formulate concepts

Observable Behaviors

- He may have difficulties with abstract reasoning. He may be quite verbal and personable and may, thus, initially impress people as normal in intellectual ability. Extended conversation, however, gradually unearths evidence of concrete thinking. As abstractions are made, the child gets lost. For example, while he may readily recognize that a tree, flower and potato all grow, he may fail to categorize them as vegetation. Or, he may recognize that Boston and Atlanta are cities but not understand why Massachusetts and Georgia are categorized as states. With conceptualization difficulties, he has trouble learning in most subject area classes.
- He may wear a blank facial expression when abstractions are discussed in class. In science he does not understand that the atmosphere is full of gases unless someone gives him concrete proof. In social studies he is lost in discussion of abstract terms such as *conservative, liberal, bourgeois.*
- He may struggle when asked to compare and contrast two or more items. He may list superficialities and fail to note major characteristics. For example, he may proudly state that both a dog and a cat have four legs and never mention that they are both animals.
- He may have poor reading comprehension. He may, in fact, be a capable decoder, impressively reading paragraphs aloud from grade-level materials; nonetheless, his comprehension of specific vocabulary and of the general text is

usually well below par.
- He may be unable to generalize. While he may understand that $3 \times 4 = 12$, he may not grasp that $4 \times 3 = 12$ as well. Or he may learn that property with those particular numbers but not generalize that $5 \times 6 = 6 \times 5$.
- He may have trouble drawing conclusions or making inferences. He does not catch the message in subtle stories and often does not understand the riddles told by his classmates.

Teaching Strategies

- Try to relate new concepts to practical experience. Use concrete materials whenever possible to demonstrate abstractions. Through simple discussions you can help the student note the linkage between concrete happenings and abstract ideas.
- Ask the student simple, direct questions whenever possible to make certain that he understands the material being presented in class.
- Help the student see how generalizations may be made in learning. Note in science, for example, that measuring sulfuric acid in a beaker is the same procedure as measuring water in a beaker. Discussing the similarities and differences in this and in other measurement procedures encourages the student to think in terms of comparisons and contrasts in all aspects of his learning.
- Offer extra practice in categorizing and classifying. Start with simple concepts, gradually increasing the level of reasoning required as the student makes progress. In social studies, the student could be asked to separate a pile of word cards according to Indian food, Indian culture, and Indian heroes. In math, the student might manipulate attribute blocks to learn concepts of size, color and shape. In English, he might separate action words (verbs) from description words (adjectives).
- Develop games and exercises to develop reasoning. Ask riddles ("What's a five-sided shape?"). Encourage the student

to bring in riddles to ask you.
- Develop a list of relevant cause-effect relationships for the student to discuss. In science, for example, he can start with *clouds-rain* and move on to more challenging word pairs as he grasps the cause-effect concept.
- Encourage the student to make judgements of time, distance, and weight. For example, ask "How tall is your mother?" "How far can you throw a ball?" "How much does a baby gerbil weigh?" Follow up by having him make the actual measurements.
- Develop a list of antonyms, and ask the student to "play opposites" during free time. In science he could be asked *sweet-sour, Fahrenheit-Celsius*; in math he might be presented with *addition-subtraction, prime-composite*.
- Develop the student's use of contextual picture and/or word clues. Remind him to really look at all available graphics for help in understanding what he reads and what he hears.
- Help him gain a better understanding of the calendar and its relatedness to everyday life. Make a game of calendar quizzing by asking such questions as "What month comes after Christmas?" "When do we get out of school for the summer?" "When is Thanksgiving?"
- Let the student know that you do not think he is stupid. Build up his self-esteem by seeing to it that he experiences success on a regular basis.

Chapter 21

DIFFICULTIES UNDERSTANDING LANGUAGE

DEFINITION OF DIFFICULTIES UNDERSTANDING LANGUAGE: difficulty understanding language that is spoken or written by others; problems relating speech and words to meaning

Observable Behaviors

- The child is apt to have had delayed speech development. He may not have listened and mimicked language accurately at the appropriate stage in his early childhood.
- He may have vocabulary problems, difficulty attaching meaning to words. He generally does not understand the subtleties of figurative language and takes phrases such as "Go fly a kite" and "I thought I'd die" quite literally.
- He may be slow to respond to verbal stimuli. Because it takes him extra time to process verbal input, he may look vague when given directions to an exercise or assignment. He may need to repeat directions to himself several times before he is able to grasp what it is that he must do.
- He may be similarly slow in peer group play, failing to understand the rules of a game or the Saturday afternoon activities plan as it unfolds. The child's language deficiency often leads to rejection by his impatient peers. He is, therefore, likely to be an isolated, lonely individual.
- He may have difficulty determining the main idea of a reading selection. While he may have little trouble decoding the actual words in the passage, he does not always grasp the central points of the material.
- He may respond more readily to spoken language when it is reinforced by gestures and visual aids.

Teaching Strategies

- Give short, simple directions whenever possible. If instructions are complex, break them down into pieces and allow the student to take one step at a time to successful accomplishment of the task.
- On homemade worksheets provide visual clues, such as pictures or diagrams, to break up the page and to reinforce the message being expressed.
- Pair the child up with a buddy who can provide him with clear, complete xeroxed notes of the class lectures. While the student should take notes on his own if possible, his language processing difficulties will make this a very trying task indeed.
- Using simple language, tape-record resource material to back up the curriculum in social studies and science. Be certain that the student has access to a manually operated tape recorder which will allow him to stop, start, and rewind as necessary for maximum absorption of the information.
- Encourage the student to keep a vocabulary notebook, subdivided by subject areas, in which he may jot down the meaning of basic vocabulary. In math class, for example, he might note terms such as *prime* and *composite*; in English, *simile*, *metaphor*.
- When presenting new procedures or concepts, start at the concrete level through manipulative devices and slowly advance to a more abstract level. Use concrete materials as often as possible to demonstrate new concepts. The student will learn most effectively through hands-on activities.
- Ask frequent, short questions to check that the student is understanding the information as it is being presented.
- Give the student credit for work completed correctly. Gently point out what has been missed.
- As a general practice beneficial to *all* students, review the previous lesson before starting a new one. This spiral approach to teaching promotes successful learning.

Chapter 22

PROBLEMS IN EXPRESSION
(Expressive language deficit)

DEFINITION OF EXPRESSIVE LANGUAGE DEFICIT: deficiency in skills required to produce language for communication with other individuals (speaking, writing)

Observable Behaviors

- The child is apt to have trouble recalling words for usage in speech. He may refer to "whatchamacallit" and "whoosit" with considerable frequency.
- He may demonstrate articulation difficulties. He may omit, substitute, distort, or add sounds in the words he produces, saying *stop* for *stopped*, *wabbit* for *rabbit*, *mith* for *miss* (lisping), or *sumber* for *summer*.
- He may use definitions for objects whose name he cannot recall. For example, he may refer to "that thing they put around a dog's neck," rather than a collar.
- He may use a rather elaborate gesture system and sound effects to offset his inability to express himself verbally.
- He may be shy and seldom talk in class or be disruptive. Both are defense mechanisms.
- He may use immature grammar or "telegraphic" speech. He may be unable to express himself in a complete sentence.
- He may appear nonfluent at times, stammering, stuttering, or using "uh" excessively.
- He may recognize correct sentence structure but not use it. The child who can correct himself after a teacher asks what is wrong with the statement, "He don't know," but cannot avoid making the mistake again may have an expressive language problem.

- He may have problems with written language as well as oral expression. He is likely to write three sentences when asked to compose a full page essay.
- He may be unable to function adequately in rapid oral drills. While he may do well in written computation and be a fine speller, he may perform poorly when asked to recite math facts or to participate in a spelling bee.

Teaching Strategies

- Gently encourage verbal responses and oral participation in class. Allow the student enough time to organize his answer mentally before requiring him to spew it out verbally. Try not to let other students in class place pressure on him to answer before he is ready. If the child has a rhythm disorder, he may require even more time to express his answer. When he is "stuck" and cannot seem to start to respond, gently ask him if it is all right to go on to someone else, and then come back to him. This relieves him of embarrassment, yet still allows him to communicate.
- Provide verbal cues and moral support, if necessary, when asking the student for oral responses. Helping him with the first syllable of a word he cannot recall or nodding with a smile as he speaks can be enormously effective in helping him cope with his problem.
- If you do not understand what the student is saying, ask him to repeat himself. If you still do not understand, ask him to try to express his idea in another way.
- If speech is the problem, try to note patterns of substitutions, omissions, additions, and/or distortions as the student speaks. Gently correct him, if possible. Refer him to a speech pathologist if the problem is severe.
- To facilitate better recall, help the student organize his notes. His chances of being able to express himself on any given topic are greater if he has overlearned the material and has it mentally organized.

- Help him learn the subtleties of idiomatic speech. Explain what it means "to be hard put to do something" or what is being asked when he is told to "shake a leg."
- Read aloud to him as often as possible. Explain idioms and figures of speech as you go along. Discuss descriptions and plot in detail.
- Teach explicit rules of sentence formation. Helping the child understand basic grammar will help his syntax. Work on oral grammar and fluency through plays, skits, and tape recorders. Encourage him to listen to and evaluate his own tape-recorded speech.
- When possible, tape-record his written work first, then have him transcribe. This is often impractical, but it can be particularly helpful in getting the student to expand his ideas for written composition.
- Be flexible about requirements for output. Occasionally allow him to produce tapes, plays, interviews, and gestures as a substitution for written work. Adjust the length of assignments according to his ability.
- Have him tell all he can about certain specific objects, using as many descriptive words as possible. Have him describe pictures from books, T.V. shows, and the plots of radio stories. Ask for a detailed plot summary with full descriptions, using many adjectives and adverbs.
- Grade according to individual performance. When possible, measure the student against himself rather than against others in the class.

Chapter 23

VISUAL IMPAIRMENTS

D EFINITION OF VISUAL IMPAIRMENTS: partial or total loss of visual acuity

Observable Behaviors

- The child is apt to have medical symptoms, such as red eyes, crusty lids and lashes, recurring styes or swollen lids, watery eyes, crossed eyes, pupils of unequal size, eyes that move excessively, or drooping eyelids.
- He may be sensitive to light.
- He may tilt his head or thrust it forward to see more easily.
- He may shut or cover one eye, or rub his eyes frequently, or blink more than usual.
- He may hold objects close to his eyes or far away to see them more clearly. He may complain of nausea or headaches following intense eye work.
- He may complain that he cannot see the blackboard from his seat in the classroom, or he may squint or frown when trying to do close work.
- He may reverse letters, syllables, or words in his reading and writing. He also may tend to confuse letters of a similar shape, such as *n* and *m* or *h* and *n*.
- He may frequently lose his place on a page while reading or writing.
- He may produce sloppy papers, with writing running off the lines and with poor spacing between letters and words.
- He may have somewhat different behavioral tendencies, if he is actually blind. He may hold his head down, as he has no need to hold it up to see, or he may hold his head down only slightly, in order to hear better. Since he cannot imitate or react to the facial expression of others, he may look

somewhat unresponsive. The blind child also tends to frequently shift his weight from one foot to the other or turn his head rapidly from side to side; this self-stimulation replaces the stimulation of normal sight.

Teaching Strategies

- Keep the aisles as clear as possible in your classroom.
- Orient the child to any obstructions and reorient him when any changes are made in the arrangement of desks or other objects in the room. Caution others in the class to keep doors all the way open or closed, to tuck wastebaskets under desks, and to be otherwise aware of the visually impaired child's need for spatial consistency.
- Be consistent about the storage of materials and the staging of activities in your classroom.
- It may be helpful to attach pictures or decals to windows and glass doors so the visually impaired student may more easily detect the presence of transparent barriers.
- Pair the student up with various children who have normal vision to help him organize his work materials, to alert him to physical obstacles in class, to help him take notes, to assist him in case of fire. Do not isolate him by assigning him to only one aide for long periods at a time.
- Provide the student with assistance when necessary but be cautious not to overprotect him. It is important that he learn to move about in his environment, to explore and to meet his own needs as often as possible. While it is sometimes physically and psychologically easier for people with normal vision to simply bring things to the visually impaired child, it is crucial that he be encouraged to go out and seek what he wants independently. Ultimately this approach will build the student's self-esteem and will help prepare him for independent living.
- Teach the student to discriminate between shapes, textures, temperatures and weights through tactile manipulation.

- Allow plenty of practice time in learning situations.
- Support the student's efforts to do whatever he has to do to see more easily and clearly. Do not draw attention to the distance at which he holds objects from his eyes.
- Provide extra supervision for the visually impaired child on field trips. Try to anticipate sensory stimulation that will occur on the trip and discuss these with the student prior to departure.
- Praise the student for his efforts and accomplishments. Remember that the visually impaired child may not be able to see smiles or gestures of approval when he has worked well. Thus it is important or provide either verbal praise or a gentle pat of satisfaction to reinforce his positive behaviors.

Chapter 24

HEARING LOSS

DEFINITION OF HEARING LOSS: partial or total loss of auditory acuity

Observable Behaviors

- The child is apt to cock his head to the side to hear more adequately.
- He may have difficulty following oral directions. He may ask for frequent repetitions of directions or instructional material, or he may be less assertive and simply resign himself to failure.
- He may be dependent upon looking at others' work before starting his own. Because he has not fully heard or understood the directions given, he may look to his classmates for visual clues to follow. He is *not* cheating.
- He may be inattentive in class. Because he cannot adequately hear what is being said, he does not understand the points being made, and, in frustration, he ultimately tunes out altogether.
- He may be either stubborn and disobedient or shy and withdrawn. The frustration of hearing either distortions or nothing at all is overwhelming and often leads to such defensive behavior.
- He may have trouble understanding the subtleties of language. Because he is very literal, he misses many of the messages conveyed in figurative speech. His subsequent failure to perceive social cues often leads to rejections by his peers, and, thus, the hearing impaired child is often an isolated and lonely person.
- He may become confused by a lot of activity in the classroom. He does not know where to affix his auditory at-

tention.
- He may lose his place during oral reading sessions in school. He may not be able to hear the points in the selection where other students are starting and stopping as they read aloud.
- He may seem to lack a sense of humor. His failure to laugh and joke is due less to a humorless nature, however, than to his inability to hear the comments that are made.
- He may have some difficulties with lipreading. Many phonemes (*P, B, M*) look alike to lipreaders; other sounds (*H, K, G, N*) cannot be seen at all.
- He may have medical symptoms such as frequent earaches, fluid running from the ears, frequent colds or sore throats, and recurring tonsilitis.

Teaching Strategies

- When the hearing impaired child first enters your class, follow a routine so that he will be able to anticipate the day's activities.
- Set realistic goals for the student. Consult his cumulative file for specific suggestions offered by specialists who have evaluated him in the past. While academic standards may vary somewhat, it is nonetheless appropriate to maintain normal expectations for the student's behavior and level of responsibility.
- Discuss the hearing loss with the child. Alert him if the volume of his speech is inappropriate or if his expressive style is too monotonous.
- Face the student whenever you speak. Seat him in a central location so that he does not have to strain to see either you or other speakers in the room. Be sure to avoid talking with your back toward the class as you write on the blackboard.
- Be aware of the student's reliance on lipreading as a visual aid. If you darken the room for the use of audiovisual equipment, leave sufficient light for lipreading. In a normally lit classroom, be cautious not to stand in front of a window to speak, as the resulting glare cast around you will diminish

the student's ability to see your lip movements.
- Speak naturally, in full sentences, rather than in single words or phrases. It is easier to grasp meaning in context than from isolated words. Remind his classmates to do the same, alerting them that careful articulation is more important than either increased volume or exaggerated speech patterns in communicating with hearing impaired individuals.
- Offer the student supplementary instructional time so that he will not fall behind. If necessary, arrange tutorials matching a hearing impaired student with one who can hear normally for sharing notes or studying for tests. Be cautious to choose a sensitive listening helper, however, one who will offer aid as necessary, but who will not foster dependency in the hearing impaired student.
- Avoid using idioms excessively. Figurative speech is very difficult to follow for the child with a hearing loss.
- Be aware of what you say and how you say it. Watch your facial expressions and body language to be sure that they match your words.
- Use diagrams and other visual aids as often as possible. Write key words or new vocabulary on the blackboard or on an overhead projector. In addition, glance or point toward persons or objects in the room whenever they are discussed.
- Provide an outline of material to be covered in class.
- Try to minimize the noise level in the room. Since a hearing aid amplifies all sound, a noisy atmosphere makes it difficult for the student to sort out important from unimportant sounds. Explain this to the other students in class.
- If a student's hearing aid seems to be malfunctioning, check the following (Gearheart and Weishahn, 1976, pp.39-40):
  - Check to make sure the battery is not dead.
  - Determine if the battery is in properly, with the positive and negative terminals in the proper position.
  - Check the cord to see if it is worn or broken or if the receiver is cracked.

- Check to be sure the plug-in points are not loose. Check both the hearing aid and the receiver.
- Check the ear mold to make sure it is not obstructed by wax and that it is inserted properly. An improperly fitted ear mold can cause irritation and feedback (squeaky sounds).
- Keep a fresh battery at school (changed at least monthly, even though it may not have been used) so that the child does not have to go without his hearing aid on the day the battery goes dead. Often the resource/itinerant teacher will have an extra supply of batteries and will assist in determining where other problems might exist.

- There are some additional considerations that the regular teacher must be aware of with respect to proper care and maintenance of hearing aids.
- Do not get the hearing aid wet.
- Serious damage may result from leaving it in extremely hot or cold places.
- Always turn the aid off before removing it from the ear. Removing the aid without turning the aid off will cause a squeal.
- Do not allow the child to wear the hearing microphone too close to the receiver; if this is done, the aid will make unusual noises. If the child has a unilateral loss (one ear), the hearing aid should be worn on the opposite side of the receiver.
- Do not take the aid apart and attempt to repair it. This should be done by a hearing aid dealer.
- If the student requires interpreting, seat the interpreter near you. This will allow the student to keep an eye on both of you at once.
- To get the child's attention, gently tap him on the shoulder, trying not to startle him. Calling out his name generally will not help.
- Frequently double check that the student has understood your major points. Ask review questions on a regular basis.

- Encourage the student to be assertive, to ask for repetitions or explanations whenever the need arises.
- Be aware that hearing impaired children generally fatigue more easily than others due to the constant strain of compensating. Allow rest periods or individual work time on a regular basis.
- Reinforce the student frequently for his efforts.

Appendix A

A FINAL NOTE to TEACHERS

THE manual you have just read presents a framework for understanding and educating the student with special learning needs. It has presented a basic introduction to learning styles, to task analysis, to common diagnostic measures, and to numerous categories of specific learning problems. For the sake of clarity, the latter were presented as discreet chapters, each individually defined and with separate suggestions of teaching strategies. In real life, however, students have unique *combinations* of difficulties that cannot be neatly categorized with any one label and that cannot be treated with any one set of teaching techniques. And in real life, classrooms often have unique combinations of situational difficulties that impede adequate individualization. Therefore, in reality, teachers may only be expected to do the best they can to meet the individual needs of all students at all times.

You will find that many of the strategies listed in this manual could be used effectively for a variety of learning problems in your classroom, but you will also find that certain suggestions would be more useful to you if they were modified. I urge you to be inventive, to use this handbook as a framework for developing your *own* individualized approach to mainstreaming. In addition, I encourage you to read any of the dozens of further books and materials on individualization.

And finally, I suggest that you discuss your readings and your thoughts on mainstreaming with a colleague who can offer the professional and emotional support that will be so helpful as you accept students with learning problems into your mainstreamed classroom.

Appendix B

ASSESSING CLASSROOM LEARNING

STUDENTS with learning problems generally suffer greatly in classroom testing situations. They find themselves face to face with impossible time limits, with lengthy questions which must be read, with numerous essay answers which must be written, with threats of points lost for misspellings. They become tense and anxious and generally cannot demonstrate the full extent of their knowledge in the subject area being tested. Therefore, it is clear that along with individualization in curriculum planning must come an individualized approach to evaluation of student progress.

There are two levels of memory that are tapped in tests of classroom learning: recognition and recall.

Recognition refers to the ability to choose the correct answer from a pool of available visual or auditory responses. Formats of tests of recognition include multiple-choice items; matching sections; and short-answer questions, when the answers are listed elsewhere on the page.

Recall refers to the ability to pull a fact from one's memory, unaided by the availability of visual or auditory choices. Formats of tests of recall include fill-in-the-blank sections, essay items, and short-answer questions. True-False items fall somewhere between recognition and recall in classification.

Most teachers tend to weight their tests more heavily toward recall than recognition items, requiring students to memorize vast amounts of information quite needlessly. While recall of facts and figures may frequently be desirable, there is much information that need not be memorized to be adequately learned. Therefore, it is suggested that teachers develop tests that provide a good balance of recognition and recall items. For example, an exam might include ten matching items, five essays, and ten short-answer questions, with the list of possible answers written above.

PREPARING TESTS

There are several further points to keep in mind as teachers prepare tests of classroom learning.

(1) The physical presentation of the test is very important.
- Try not to cram too much writing on one page, as this creates visual figure-ground difficulties and is psychologically intimidating to even the stronger students.
- Type or legibly print the test. Many students miss items simply because they cannot read the teacher's handwriting.
- Use caution when mimeographing test papers on both sides. The ink often bleeds, making it extremely difficult for the student to decipher the content.

(2) Be sure to leave enough work space for the students. Math examples, for instance, should not be overcrowded on one page. Students will compute more accurately if examples are well spaced, particularly if lines are drawn in to delineate the work area for each individual item. Provide long enough blanks for students with fine motor difficulties to write their complete responses to short-answer questions and enough blank space for them to adequately express their ideas in essays.

(3) Avoid shortcuts when making up tests. Unnecessary abbreviations and ditto marks may confuse the student.

(4) Provide clear, concise directions. It is often helpful to read them aloud to the class. Those who do not need this assistance will move ahead and begin working on the test; those who do will be more likely to follow the directions accurately than they would if they were left

to read the instructions on their own.

(5) Test for understanding of concepts rather than for mastery of writing mechanics. Many learning disabled students are able to learn the necessary information for a test but present it poorly in writing. If spelling and punctuation must "count," grade them separately from content learning. When students are confident that teachers will provide corrections without grading off for mechanical errors, they are more relaxed and tend to fare better in test situations.

Modifications of Tests

Students with learning problems may require modifications of the tests adminstered to the rest of the class. There are numerous ways by which their special needs may be addressed. Some teachers make up two versions of the same test, designing one specifically for the students in class who have difficulties with reading or writing. They hand out both at the same time, camouflaging the fact that there are two sets of expectations being addressed in an exam period.

Other teachers construct one test for all, with only every second or third item being appropriate for the student with special needs. While the rest of the class must complete the entire test, the learning disabled student is quietly instructed to answer the even-numbered items and to approach the others only if he cares to try.

It sometimes helps to provide the student with a helper who can read the test aloud either in a quiet corner or off in another room. The helper may simply read the questions, letting the student respond independently, or may read the questions and take dictation as the student recites his answer.

Teachers may choose to modify only certain sections of a test. For example, they may require all students to complete the True-False and matching items but make allowances on the essay questions. On the latter, students may be required to write only two or three full sentences or may be asked to write a full answer in outline form.

Many students would actually be able to complete the unmodified test if it were not for the time constraints of a normal class period. These students are best served by being invited back after school or during a study hall to finish their work.

BIBLIOGRAPHY

Abbott, Jean: *Classroom Strategies to Aid the Disabled Learner*, Cambridge, MA, Educators Publishing Service, 1978.

Aiello, Barbara (Ed.): *Making it Work: Practical Ideas for Integrating Exceptional Children into Regular Classrooms*, Reston, VA, Council for Exceptional Children, 1975.

Aiello, Barbara: *Mainstreaming: What it is and What to do about it*. Palo Alto, CA Education Today, 1977.

Alonso, L., Moor, P.M., Raynor, S.: *Mainstreaming Preschoolers: Children with Visual Handicaps*, U.S. Dept. of HEW Publication number (OHDS) 78-31112.

Birch, Jack W.: *Hearing Impaired Children in the Mainstream*, Minneapolis, Leadership Training Institute of Univ. of Minnesota, 1975.

Blakenship, Colleen and Lilly, M. Stephen: *Mainstreaming Students With Learning and Behavior Problems*, New York, Holt, Rinehart, & Winston, 1981.

Chaiken, William E.: *Mainstreaming the Learning Disabled Adolescent: A Staff Development Guide*. Springfield, IL, Charles C Thomas, Publisher, 1979.

Clarke, C., Callender, J., and Migdail, S.: *A Teacher's Notebook: Alternatives for Children with Learning Problems*, Boston, National Assoc. of Independent Schools, 1975.

Cruickshank, William M.: *Learning Disabilities: The Struggle From Adolescence Toward Adulthood*. Syracuse, NY, Syracuse University Press, 1980.

Farrold, Robert, and Schamber, Richard: *Diagnostic and Prescriptive Techniques*, SD, Adapt Press, 1973.

Fisher, Johanna: *A Parents' Guide To Learning Disabilities*, New York, Scribner's, 1978.

Hart, Verna: *Mainstreaming Children with Special Needs*, New York, Longman, 1981.

Hayes, Marnell: *Oh Dear, Somebody Said "Learning Disabilities!"* San Rafael, CA, Academic Therapy, 1975.

Integration of Children with Special Needs in a Regular Classroom, Lexington, MA, Lexington Teacher Training Project, 1974.

Jordan, June B.: *Teacher, Please Don't Close the Door: the Exceptional Child in the Mainstream*, Reston, VA, Council for Exceptional Children, 1976.

Lerner, Janet: *Children with Learning Disabilities*, (2nd ed.), New York, Houghton-Mifflin, 1976.

Lowenbraun, Sheila: *Teaching the Slow Learning Child*, Columbus, OH, Merrill, 1976.

Lynn, Roa: *Learning Disabilities: An Overview of Theories, Approaches, and Politics*, New York, Free Press, 1979.

MacDonald, R.L.: *Teaching the Slow Learning Child*, CA, Media Informational Systems, 1972.

Mager, R.F.: *Preparing Instructional Objectives*, (2nd ed.), Belmont, CA, Fearon, 1975.

Mann, Philip, and Sinter, Patricia: *Handbook in Diagnostic Teaching*, Boston, Allyn and Bacon, 1974.
McCarthy, James, and McCarthy, Joan: *Learning Disabilities*, Boston, Allyn and Bacon, 1974.
McLoughlin, James A., Lewis, Rena B.: *Assessing Special Students: Strategies and Procedures*, Columbus, OH, Merrill, 1981.
Orlansky, J.Z.: *Mainstreaming the Hearing Impaired Child: An Educational Alternative*, Austin, Learning Concepts, 1977.
Paul, J.L., Turnbull, A.P., and Cruickshank, W.M.: *Mainstreaming: A Practical Guide*, New York, Schocken, 1979.
Student Learning Styles: Diagnosing and Prescribing Programs: National Association of Secondary School Principals, 1979.
Valett, Robert: *The Remediation of Learning Disabilities*, Belmont, CA, Fearon, 1967.
Van Osdol, B.M., Van Osdol, W., and Shane, D.: *Learning Disabilities, K-12 Manual*, Idaho, Idaho Research Foundation, 1974.

TESTS REFERRED TO IN THIS TEXT

Brigance Diagnostic Inventory of Essential Skills, by Albert H. Brigance, Woburn, MA, Curriculum Associates, Inc., 1981.
Detroit Tests of Learning Aptitude, by Harry J. Baker and Bernice Leland, Indianapolis, Bobbs-Merrill, 1967.
Gates-MacGinitie Reading Tests, 2nd edition, by Walter H. MacGinitie, New York, Teachers College Press, 1978.
Gilmore Oral Reading Test by John V. Gilmore and Ewaice C. Gilmore, New York, Harcourt Brace Jovanovich, Inc., 1968.
Key Math Diagnostic Arithmetic Test, by Austin J. Connelly, William Nachtman, and E. Milo Pritchett, Circle Pines, MN, American Guidance Service, Inc., 1971.
Peabody Individual Achievement Test, by Lloyd M. Dunn and Frederick C. Markwardt, Jr., Circle Pines, MN, American Guidance Service, Inc., 1970.
Illinois Test of Psycholinguistic Abilities, by Samuel A. Kirk, James J. McCarthy, and Winifred D. Kirk, Urbana, IL, U. of Illinois Press, 1968.
Wechsler Intelligence Scale for Children-Revised (WISC-R), by David Wechsler, New York, The Psychological Corporation, 1974.
Wide Range Achievement Test, by Joseph F. Jastak, Sidney W. Bijou, and Sarah Jastak, Wilmington, DE, Jastak Associates, Inc., 1978.

GLOSSARY

Auditory perception:
    ability to interpret or organize the sensory data received through the ears

Automatization:
    making repetitive and routine aspects of a task become automatic habits that require little or no conscious awareness or attention

Conceptual disorder:
    a disturbance in the ability to form abstractions of student performance on specific tasks, under specific conditions, with specific criteria for success

Criterion-referenced tests:
    direct measures to compare a student's performance to some criterion rather than to the performance of other students

Cross-modality perception:
    neurological process of converting information received through one input modality to another system within the brain

Discrimination:
    ability to distinguish one stimulus from another

Distractibility:
    supersensitivity to both internal and external stimuli

Expressive language skills:
    skills required to produce language for communication with other individuals, i.e. speaking and writing

Figure-ground distortion:
    inability to focus on an object itself without having the background or setting interfere with perception

Hyperactivity:
: persistent, heightened, and sustained activity levels that are situationally and socially inappropriate

Hyperkinesis:
: constant and excessive movement and motor activity

IEP:
: Individualized Educational Plan, developed by an Evaluation Team to meet the individual educational requirements of a student with special needs

Informal Inventories:
: informal diagnostic measures that help teachers determine a student's achievement level in relation to the actual curriculum being utilized

Impulsivity:
: behavioral characteristic of acting upon impulse without consideration of the consequences of an action

Kinesthetic learning:
: learning through motion/movement

Laterality:
: awareness of the two sides of one's body and the ability to identify them correctly as left or right (Mixed laterality is the shifting from left to right for certain activities)

Mainstreaming:
: providing each child with the most appropriate education in the least restrictive environment

Memory:
: ability to store and retrieve upon demand previously experienced sensations and perceptions; when the stimulus that originally evoked them is no longer present, it is *Recall*; when the stimulus is still present, it is *Recognition Memory*

Modality:
: channel through which an individual receives information and thereby learns

Norm-referenced tests:
: samples of student behavior under standardized condi-

tions, allowing comparison of one student's test performance to the performance of a normal group of age or grade peers

Observation:
an informal assessment technique; watching a student's behavior for diagnostic patterns

Perception:
process of organizing or interpreting the raw data obtained through the senses

Perceptual disorder:
disturbance in the awareness of objects, relations, or qualities involving the interpretation of sensory stimulation

Perceptually handicapped:
term applied to the person who has difficulty learning because of a disturbance in his perception of sensory stimuli

Perceptual-motor:
term describing the interaction of the various channels of perception with motor activity

Perseveration:
tendency to continue a specific act, behavior or attitude when it is acknowledged to no longer be appropriate to the situation at hand

Receptive language:
language that is spoken or written by others and received by the individual, i.e. listening and reading

Sensory-motor:
combination of the input of sensations and the output of motor activity

Tactile learning:
feeling and discerning through touch

Task analysis:
technique of carefully examining a particular task to discover the elements it comprises and the processes required to perform it; may be functional or structural in nature

Visual-motor (eye-hand) coordination:
>ability to coordinate vision with the movements of the body or parts of the body

Visual-spatial ability:
>ability to relate oneself in space and ability to relate sets of objects in space to each other

Visual perception:
>identification, organization, and interpretation of sensory data received by the individual through the eye

Work sample analysis:
>an informal assessment technique; examining a student's performance on a task; analyzing correct responses or errors for diagnosis of the student's strengths and weaknesses in learning

INDEX

A

Auditory discrimination, definition, 12
Auditory discrimination deficit
 definition, 68
 observable behaviors, 68-69
 related teaching strategies, 69-70
Auditory figure-ground discrimination,
 definition, 13
Auditory figure-ground discrimination
 problems
 definition, 71
 observable behaviors, 71
 related teaching strategies, 72
Auditory learner, 9
Auditory memory, definition, 12-13
Auditory memory deficit
 definition, 73
 observable behaviors, 73-74
 related teaching strategies, 74-75
Auditory motor tasks, 15
Automatization difficulties
 definition, 65
 observable behaviors, 65-66
 related teaching strategies, 66-67

B

Brigance Diagnostic Inventory of Essential Skills, 42

C

Case study, 49
Conceptualization difficulties
 definition, 91
 observable behaviors, 91-92

 related teaching strategies, 92-93
Criterion-referenced tests, 42-43, 45-46
Cross-modality functioning, 15
Cumulative records, reading and interpreting
 family data, 24
 grade patterns, 25
 IQ testing, 26
 other diagnostic testing, 27-43
 reasons for onset of problems, 24
 schools attended, 25
 student's medical history, 25
 teacher and guidance reports, 26

D

Detroit Tests of Learning Aptitude, 28-29
 the tests and specific mental faculties,
  fig. 3, 29
 sample protocol, *fig. 4,* 30
Dexadrine®, 25
Dilantin®, 25
Distractibility
 definition, 55
 observable behaviors, 55
 related teaching strategies, 56-57

E

Education for All Handicapped Children Act, xi, 5.
 evaluation meetings, 7
 evaluation procedures, 5-8
 preevaluation conference, 5
 role of parents, 6, 7
 role of team members, 5-6
Educational plan (*see* Individual Educa-

tional Plan)

F

Fine motor coordination, 14
Formal reports of evaluations, 27
Functional task analysis
  definition, 21
  sample, 22

G

Gates-MacGinitie Reading Test, 39-40
  sample protocol, *fig. 9*, 40
Gilmore Oral Reading Test, 36-37
  sample protocol, *fig. 8*, 37
Gray Oral Reading Test, 36
Gross motor coordination, 14

H

Hearing loss
  definition, 102
  observable behaviors, 102, 103
  related teaching strategies, 103-106
Hyperactivity
  definition, 60
  observable behaviors, 60-61
  related teaching strategies, 61-62

I

Illinois Test of Psycholinguistic Abilities, 40-42
  sample profile, *fig. 10*, 41
Impulsivity
  definition, 58
  observable behaviors, 58
  related teaching strategies, 59
Individual Educational Plan (IEP), procedures to develop, 5-7
Informal assessments
  criterion-referenced tests, 45-46
  inventories, 46-47
  observation, 44-45
  work sample analysis, 45

Informal inventories
  steps for designing, 46-47
  suggestions for use, 47-48

K

Key Math Diagnostic Arithmetic Test, 33
Kinesthetic learning, 14-15

L

Language difficulties
  problems in expression, 96-98
  problems understanding language, 94-95
Learning disabilities, characteristics of moderate, xii-xiii
Least restrictive environment, 7

M

McLoughlin and Lewis, 20, 21, 38, 46
Mainstreaming, definition, xi
Memory, 108
Modalities
  auditory modality, 11-13
  cross-modality functioning, 15
  kinesthetic learning, 14-15
  motor functioning, 13-15
  tactile stimulation, 14
  visual modality, 10-11

O

Observation, 44-45
  checksheet, xv

P

Peabody Individual Achievement Test (PIAT), 32-33
  sample protocol, *fig. 5*, 32
Perception, 9-10
Perseveration
  definition, 63
  related teaching strategies, 63-64

Index

Public Law 94-142 (*see* Educational for All Handicapped Children Act)

R

Ritalin®, 25

S

Standardized tests, norm-referenced
  Detroit Tests of Learning Aptitude, 28-29
  Gates-MacGinitie Reading Test, 39-40
  Gilmore Oral Reading Test, 36
  Gray Oral Reading Test, 36
  Illinois Test of Psycholinguistic Abilities (ITPA), 40-42
  Key Math Diagnostic Arithmetic Test, 33
  Peabody Individual Achievement Test (PIAT), 32-33
  Wepman Auditory Discrimination Test, 31-32
  Wide Range Achievement Test (WRAT), 33-34
  Woodcock Reading Mastery Tests, 36-39
Structural task analysis, 19-20
  sample, 20

T

Tactile stimulation, 14
Task analysis
  structural task analysis, 19-20
  functional task analysis, 21-22
Tests of classroom learning, 108-111
  preparation of 109-110
  modification of 110-111

V

Visual discrimination, definition, 10
Visual discrimination deficits
  definition, 76
  observable behaviors, 76-77
  related teaching strategies, 77-78
Visual figure-ground discrimination, definition, 11
Visual figure-ground difficulties
  definition, 79
  observable behaviors, 79-80
  related teaching strategies, 80-81
Visual impairments
  definition, 99
  observable behaviors, 99-100
  related teaching strategies, 100-101
Visual Learner, 9
Visual memory, definition, 11
Visual memory deficits
  definition, 82
  observable behaviors, 82-83
  related teaching strategies, 83-85
Visual-motor abilities, 15
Visual-motor deficits
  definition, 86
  observable behaviors, 86
  related teaching strategies, 86-97
Visual-spatial relationship difficulties
  definition, 88
  observable behaviors, 88-89
  related teaching strategies, 89-90

W

Wechsler Intelligence Scale for Children-Revised (WISC-R), 26-27
  intelligence classifications, *fig. 2,* 27
Wepman Auditory Discrimination Test, 31-32
Wide Range Achievement Test (WRAT), 33, 34
  sample spelling protocol, *fig. 6,* 34
  sample reading protocol, *fig. 7,* 35
Woodcock Reading Mastery Tests, 36-39
Work sample analysis, 45